## Praise for
## *A World Champion's Guide to Running the Beer Mile*

"Lewis Kent, and the current crop of competitive beer milers, has taken a traditional distance runner's rite of passage and transformed it into a professional sport—and it's entertaining as hell. Kent's story is as fascinating and fun as watching your first beer mile. It's also loaded with plenty of tips and tricks for the aspiring beer miler, which is great because you'll know doubt want to lace 'em up and drink some down after reading. I'd recommend grabbing a cold one and enjoying this read in one binge session."

—Desiree Linden, two-time Olympic marathoner and winner of the 2018 Boston Marathon

"When you hear about the Beer Mile and see how these guys do it, in the time they do it in, it's undeniably fascinating. Most of us can't drink four beers in five minutes on the couch. These guys run a mile. Hear the account from one of the guys who became the best in the world at a niche sport that has fascinated North America."

—Darren Rovell, Senior Executive Producer, The Action Network

"Running a beer mile is a uniquely painful (yet fun!) experience. It requires exceptional running AND chugging skills, along with an iron stomach and care free attitude. Few have done it better than Lewis Kent and the advice he puts forth in these pages is rock solid."

—Nick Symmonds, six-time US 800m champion and CEO of Run Gun

# A WORLD CHAMPION'S GUIDE TO RUNNING THE BEER MILE

## A MANUAL AND MEMOIR OF RUNNING, CHUGGING, AND (NOT) THROWING UP

## LEWIS KENT

Skyhorse Publishing

Skyhorse Publishing books may be purchased in bulk at special discounts for sales promotion, corporate gifts, fund-raising, or educational purposes. Special editions can also be created to specifications. For details, contact the Special Sales Department, Skyhorse Publishing, 307 West 36th Street, 11th Floor, New York, NY 10018 or info@skyhorsepublishing.com.

Skyhorse® and Skyhorse Publishing® are registered trademarks of Skyhorse Publishing, Inc.®, a Delaware corporation.

Visit our website at www.skyhorsepublishing.com.

10 9 8 7 6 5 4 3 2 1

Library of Congress Cataloging-in-Publication Data is available on file.

Cover design by Tom Lau
Cover photo credit: Caleb Kerr

Print ISBN: 978-1-5107-3555-2
Ebook ISBN: 978-1-5107-3556-9

Printed in the United States of America.

# Table of Contents

# Author's Note

I was just your regular college kid who liked to run and drink beer; I never thought to put the two together. This is my story of how sometimes extraordinary things happen to ordinary people.

# CHAPTER ONE

# Twenty-Four Hours

"Lewis, I have the *Ellen* show calling me asking for your contact information . . . What's going on?" Guy Schultz, my university cross country coach had called me, exasperated. I just laughed in response. After all, I had interrupted a live photo shoot with the Discovery Channel to take his call. How can I explain this one?

I had just broken the Beer Mile World Record in 4:51 and the media was on fire. I had done over thirty interviews in three days. I was waking up at 6:00 a.m. to go on morning radio, leaving university lectures to take calls from ESPN, you name it. I had already booked my flight to Austin, Texas for the World Championships on December 1, 2015, and was training hard for it.

Word came through that Ellen DeGeneres wanted me to go on her show, but it would have to be taped in Burbank,

California the day before the World Championships in Austin, Texas. It would ultimately play out to be the craziest twenty-four hours of my life.

My older brother, Jordan, and teammate, Phil, were booked to travel with me to Austin. Their support, and that of a man named Kris, kept me sane in what would quickly unfold into an insane trip.

We landed in Austin, Texas at 2:25 p.m. on November 27. I had been in Austin for the Beer Mile World Championships before, but back then, nobody knew who I was. This time it was different; I was now the world record holder, and all eyes were on me to take down the current world champion, Corey Gallagher. The media frenzy surrounding the event was intense already, and I knew that *The Ellen Show* would introduce the sport to a whole new demographic on the very day that the World Championships would be broadcasted live by FloTrack.

I had been running since the age of ten and had been pretty competitive locally, but by no means had I made the leap to the elite level. While the Olympics were not in my future, I was a proud varsity runner for the University of Western Ontario in London, Ontario.

I knew enough about how elite athletes prepared, and I took my training very seriously. Although the beer mile was a fun and recreational event for most, there was a growing group of runners who had been taking it more seriously as well. Being one of the favorites, I wanted to do well. I wasn't there to finish second.

FloTrack had organized a professional, world-class event. (For those who don't know, FloTrack is one of the largest companies in the United States for covering live track and field and running events, with hundreds of thousands of viewers for big events such as NCAA's and the US Track and Field Championships.) With major media interviews, lots of online presence, countless talks with radio shows and meetings with sponsors, this was a real World Championships in every aspect. And as such, the organizers had not banked on their headline athlete and top-seed leaving Austin two days before the race. So when I told them I wouldn't be around the two days leading up to the event, they were hesitant. However, once I told them the reason why, their feelings quickly changed as they would obviously benefit from the national media exposure as well. Arriving back late the night before the big race was far from ideal, but that is the way it had to be.

Ellen's staff had planned to tape the show on Monday, November 30, so Jordan and I left Austin and landed in LA on Sunday afternoon. There we met up with Kris Mychasiw, who had landed fifteen minutes before us. Kris was one of the most established track and field agents in Canada, known for working with Bruny Surin, a Canadian track-and-field Olympic gold medalist. Kris had seen my story and called me to see if we could work together. (He is really to blame for all of this.)

It was Kris who connected me with Brooks, coordinated the first ever professional beer mile contract, and then floated the story to Ellen. It was good to meet him in person at last and to discover that we both had the same approach to life in general. He wasn't the Jerry Maguire type; just a good guy who was seeing one of his dreams coming true: landing an athlete on *Ellen*. To my understanding, there had only been one other track athlete on *Ellen* previously: Usain Bolt. Kris was there to soak it in. Thankfully for me, as the trip unfolded, he kept me calm.

Once the three of us were together, the craziness began.

Have you ever seen those celebrities with a driver waiting at the airport in the limo, holding up a sign with their name? The guy who met us was doing just that, and I can only describe him as Lurch from *The Addams Family*. Jordan and I cracked up on the spot; this was Hollywood!

The three of us jumped into the limo and off we went. About an hour later, we arrived at our hotel, and I could only imagine all the stars who had taken the same trip and walked through the same doors. Kris walked up to the check-in counter, and when prompted for his last name, he replied, "It's pronounced like a cashew from McDonald's, Mychasiw." Jordan and I got a good laugh out of it, and I was slightly embarrassed as I had been saying it wrong for weeks. When I gave my last name, the hotel receptionist said there was a delivery left for me, pulling out two massive boxes. Excited to see what it could be, Kris joined Jordan and me in our room to open them up. One box had six brand-new pairs of Brooks shoes—two for me, one for each of the producers, as well as a pair for Ellen herself. The other box was packed with apparel. Once again, there was some stuff for Ellen and her staff, but also two shirts each for Kris, Jordan, and me. Brooks hooked us up big time.

Because we were quite a distance from nearby restaurants, and couldn't be bothered to take a shuttle or taxi, the three of us decided to have dinner at the hotel. As soon as we got there, we could tell that we were a bit out of our league because this place was *fancy*. I didn't dare look at the prices and ordered a pretty standard pasta dish. You always have to keep the stomach happy leading into a race. However, I did enjoy a luxury with dinner that most athletes avoid close to competition—a nice cold beer.

I got to know Kris better as we ate, and we immediately

clicked. I thought back to the first time I had ever spoken to him on the phone, and how he'd said the sky was the limit since the beer mile as a sport was just getting started. When he mentioned sponsorships, major media outlets, and live television, I honestly thought he was out of his mind. But now, every single thing he had mentioned had become a reality. After dinner, we decided to call it an early night as the next day was going to be a big one. Jordan and I watched some sports highlights for an hour then went to bed.

We got up early on Monday morning. The plan was to get picked up at 2:00 p.m., tape the show, and catch a 7:00 p.m. flight back to Austin, via Phoenix, landing in Texas around 2:00 a.m. This was not ideal leading into any race, and certainly not the preparation of an elite athlete for a World Championships, but how often does an opportunity to be on *Ellen* come around?

However, my focus was still on Tuesday and the big race, so I had to go running. Out I went in my Brooks gear on the streets of LA. I had planned a six-mile shake out run at an easy pace. The hotel was located at the top of a hill that must have been two miles long, so the thought of having to run back up deterred me from running down it in the first place. I settled for running laps in a parking garage about half a mile down the road. My legs were feeling great, just as they should feel before a big race. Every lap, I would pass by a few people looking for their cars. I would give a friendly nod, which they acknowledged with a bizarre, confused nod back. *Why is this kid running laps in a parking garage?* If only they knew what my next twenty-four hours looked like. Ten minutes into the run, Kris called me and told me to get back to the hotel immediately—the limo had come early to pick us up and we absolutely could not be late.

I sprinted back to the hotel as quickly as I could. With no time for a shower, I stuck my head under the bathroom sink, dried off my sweat with a towel, and got on my fresh, new Brooks kit so I would look sharp on screen. The three of us jumped into the limo. Lurch looked like he had run a few beer miles himself the night before with bags under his eyes and his hair all over the place. Chuckling amongst ourselves, off to Burbank we went.

Going in, the plan was that I would be the first guest recorded in the show's lineup so that I would have plenty of time to catch my flight. We pulled into Warner Bros. Studios—where *Ellen* shoots—and it was literally just like the movies. Our limo stopped at a gated entry where Lurch spoke with security for a minute before we continued through. It wasn't until we pulled up outside *Ellen's* building that it all started to seem real.

I was taken to a room that had one of those massive mirrors fully surrounded by dozens of light bulbs and a director's chair. The producers came in to introduce themselves, and the bundle of nerves that had been gradually collecting in my stomach instantly disappeared. They knew how big of a moment this was for a twenty-one-year-old college student and assured me it would go just fine.

A staff member asked what I would like for lunch, and when I asked what the options were, I was glad to hear, "Anything you want." Then I immediately remembered I would have to stick to my staple in the days leading up to a big race: Nutella sandwiches. (More on this later.) It was too great of a risk eating something new so close to the big race. However, this didn't stop Jordan and Kris from ordering the most extravagant lunch I have ever seen. It took all my will-power not to dive into the tacos, quesadillas, and the other mouth-watering foods they ordered. In the end, I was glad someone could take advantage of the awesome service while I dug into three Nutella sandwiches.

After lunch, I was told to remain in my room and not try to find the other guests . . . but that wasn't going to happen. This was my one shot to meet three celebrities I would never see again, and I just wasn't going to pass that up. What would they do if I got caught—give me a quick slap on the wrist and send me back to my green room? After all, it's easier to beg for forgiveness than to ask for permission.

So I left Kris and Jordan in the room and tiptoed around the halls of the studio, peeking around corners to see who was there. Full of adrenaline, I read the signs on every door, hoping to run into someone famous. Although the studio didn't look that big from the outside, inside it was a maze. There were long hallways and massive rooms packed full of people for everything from makeup to video editing. Knowing major celebrities were close by, I continued my search. Unfortunately, I got lost. Luckily, no harm was done, and I managed to find my way back just in time to meet the producer for a run-through of the course. I acted like I had just been in my green room the entire time, sitting back and watching TV. The twenty-one-year-old Canadian kid who is sponsored to drink beer and run couldn't possibly disobey direct orders, could he?

The show staff had lined up a course that meandered around and through the studio. Here was the drill: chug a beer and run a strip of the parking lot. Chug a beer and run into the studio, through a back entrance, and down the stairs in between the live audience. There, Ellen would be standing with the final beer. Whoever finishes first would be the winner of the first ever *Ellen* Beer Mile. The competitors would be me . . . and the famous Andy Zenor, a popular producer on the show.

For the run-through, the producers asked me to run the course full speed using water so they could time it and make sure it went smoothly. The course was not at all what I was used to. In a standard beer mile, there are 400 meters between beers, not the 150 meters that was mapped out. The *Ellen* Beer Mile was really a 300-meter sprint with a few beers along the way. What would happen if I threw up? I had seen my fair share of people puke in the middle of a beer mile, and while entertaining, I knew it was far from a pretty sight. The pressure of a live audience, as well as the projected fifty million viewers watching at home, didn't make it any easier. Ellen's team had flown me in and given me the full celebrity treatment for two minutes of entertainment; I knew that I had to come through on that, but the idea of throwing up my lunch in front of hundreds of middle-aged women in the audience didn't seem appealing.

The rehearsal went well, but then things changed. Why? I don't know. Now, Wanda Sykes would be interviewed first, and then Kunal Nayyar. He would be followed by a live performance by Sia, and then a portion of Ellen's famous "12 Days of Giveaways." My segment was now being recorded last. Even though it would now be a time crunch to make my flight, I was surprisingly calm; focusing on the race the next day kept my mind off the biggest appearance I had ever made.

I will never forget the few brief moments backstage before meeting Ellen. I took a quick photo for the show's official Snapchat and off I went. Stepping on stage to "Bottoms Up" by Trey Songz made me laugh; it was fitting for the occasion.

I was ready to go. I knew some of the questions Ellen would ask me, and I was ready with my key messages.

So much for that plan.

First question: "How old are you?" (Which made sense

considering I was about to chug three beers in front of day-time TV America.)

Second question: "So what is a beer mile?" No problem with that.

The third question was unplanned and caught me completely off guard: "So when do you throw up?" That cracked me up as well as the audience, but both Ellen and the crowd got an even better laugh when I told them you had to do an extra penalty lap if you threw up during the race.

After the brief interview, it was time to race. I had no idea what all the moms in the audience would think of what we were about to do, but when Ellen introduced Andy, the crowd roared, and off we went. As soon I was backstage and off camera, I tossed my sweatpants and top to Jordan while being urged by Andy that we needed to get to the course. Now in my Brooks racing kit, we jogged out the back door of the studio. The producers made sure my mic was on properly and working. They wanted the live audience to hear every sound that was about to be made in the flurry of sprinting and chugging beer. Andy gave me a quick, slightly panicked look that said, "What am I about to do?" I just chuckled. He had no idea what he was in for. Drinking and running when done in isolation is one thing, but putting them together is a completely different story.

Before sounding the air horn to start the race, someone ran into the studio next door to make sure they weren't recording. It was no big deal, just Woody Allen directing a movie; but they weren't shooting at the moment. Before I knew it, Ellen asked us if we were ready and off we went. It turned out Andy was a pretty good runner and drinker; I was barely ahead after beer number one. I managed to get a bit of a gap on the run to beer number two, but I was sprinting all out just to get a few yards ahead. By the time I put the second beer down, I knew it was game over for Andy. He was left behind in a whirlwind of carbonation and oxygen debt. Running into the studio, I had to go up a small set of stairs and came into the back of the room with the live audience waiting. They exploded with applause and screams as I trotted down the stairs towards Ellen. I threw my arms up to get the audience going before chugging back the third beer with ease, leaving Andy in the dust. He opened his third beer but didn't have the chance to put it to his lips before I was done. Ellen grabbed my hand and lifted it in the air like I had just won a UFC title match. The show wrapped up as Ellen gave me a hug and presented me with a trophy engraved "Winner of the *Ellen* Beer Mile" and told me I would be receiving a year's supply of my favorite beer! It is a moment I will never forget. Andy was still trying to grasp his breath and keep all the beer down, and the crowd, as well as Ellen, seemed to love it all. It all felt surreal.

Throughout the day, it occurred to me that the entire *Ellen* team was amazing, and Ellen herself truly was the same person off-screen as you see on-screen: genuine, kind, and authentic. Even from my few minutes with her, I could tell she really enjoys people.

The show wrapped up, and while I knew Kris and Jordan had a blast viewing the whole thing from backstage, they were now signaling to me, frantically pointing at their watches. It was 5:30 p.m. and our flight was due to take off at 7:00 p.m., on the other side of town, with LA rush hour traffic.

Lurch pulled up as we sprinted outside. We jumped in the limo, seriously concerned that we would miss our flight. Forty-five minutes later, it was obvious we would not make it. While Kris was calling the *Ellen Show* and his office in

Montreal to book Jordan and me a later flight to Austin, I called my mom.

First, I told her to tell my dad, who was anxious around airports after missing a flight earlier in his career, to not listen, as that could have been the end of him. Parents stress at the best of times about their kids, but here I was, exhausted, more than a little tipsy, speeding through LA in a limo with Lurch, their other son, and a guy from Montreal that they did not know, about to miss a flight that would take me to what was fast becoming a globally-significant athletic event. *Sit down, Dad.* My mom has always been the voice of reason in stressful moments, and this was like no other. Before we hung up, she reassured me that even if I missed my flight, I would make it to Austin in one piece and still have a great chance to win my first world title.

Even though talking to my mom was helpful, the truth was I was still stressed out. The stress broke, however, when Kris announced that he often got travel sick, and he was starting to turn green. It was like a scene straight out of the Jim Carrey movie *The Mask.* I have literally never seen somebody so green. We could not stop the car as we were trying to get to the airport and stuck in rush hour traffic. There was no way Kris was going to make it. Just before he unleashed chunks of quesadilla, he told my brother to take out his phone. (I'll spare you and not include the pictures here.) He puked everywhere. All over the limo. All over himself. Wave after wave of travel-induced vomit cascaded all over his favorite blue blazer.

In a situation where one should be miserable, and no doubt feeling terrible, Kris managed to lighten the mood of the entire ride. He was bursting into laughter in between pukes, and Jordan and I couldn't help but laugh along. This couldn't actually be happening.

Lurch immediately got on the phone to *Ellen*: "This guy has just vomited all over my limo!" Any remaining stress that we had evaporated instantly. All three of us were cracking up. Kris was smiling more than I thought possible for someone covered in his own puke.

Despite Lurch's best efforts to get us to the airport on time, we ended up missing the plane and had to stay overnight and catch a flight at 6:00 a.m. on Tuesday to arrive in Austin at 11:30 a.m., way closer to the 9:00 p.m. race than I would have liked. As I drifted off to sleep that night, all I could think was: *I wonder if this is how Usain Bolt prepared for his Olympic run?*

# CHAPTER TWO

# What Is the Beer Mile?

"ON YOUR MARKS, GO!" The hiss of carbonation leaving a freshly opened can could be heard across the track. A woman doing her daily 10:00 p.m. jog around the local high school track heard some banter as she passed by a group of runners. It was 1990, on a crisp November evening; with temperatures near freezing, the snowy days of winter were fast approaching. Across the moonlit track, she could barely make out the outlines of about half-a-dozen runners. *What were they doing?* Before she knew it, a pack of lean young men sprinted by in a fury of burps and panting. *What the heck was going on?* Just over a minute later, they came by again, but a lot more spread out this time. When she walked by what she knew as the mile start line, she was even more perplexed. There were dozens of cans of Labatt 150 scattered across the track, half of them full, and the other half of them empty. One guy stood on the sidelines with a stopwatch, calling out splits, as if this were a serious race. *What could this possibly be?*

She waited around, and thirty seconds later, a runner appeared. He scooped a beer off the track, and before she could count to ten, he had opened and chugged the beer, tilting it over his head before sprinting off again. A few moments later, another runner came sprinting by. The figure with the stopwatch yelled, "Get the beer down, Jimmy! You can still catch him!" That runner chugged a beer and took off for another lap.

She walked away puzzled, leaving the beer-soaked track more confused than a beginner trying to solve a Rubik's Cube. What she didn't know was that she just witnessed one of the first ever beer miles, a sport that just over twenty years later would end up in major media headlines across the world.

At some point in life, pretty much everyone has run a lap around a track, whether for fun or forced to do it by that annoying PE teacher who thought you needed to be more active. (You know, the old guy who once could have covered a mile in damn close to five minutes but now took that long to get from the couch to the front door? That guy.) No matter who you are, almost everyone knows the feeling of running 400 meters around the oval. Most people have also drank a beer, or at least tasted one at some point. The beer mile is the creation of four Canadian collegiate athletes who had done more than enough of both. Welcome to the history of the beer mile.

The first documented beer mile was run at Burlington High, located in Burlington, Ontario, during the early nineties. It was organized by a group of cross-country runners from Queen's University in Ontario as an offseason challenge between teammates. While the exact participants and results from that race are clouded in beer-soaked memories, the men that ran four laps and chugged four beers that day could never have imagined what they were laying the foundation for. Fast forward to 1992: enter John Markell. As an engineering student and cross-country athlete, John was an extremely high-functioning freshman whose schedule looked a little something like this: run, study, run, sleep. Repeat. Then find time to enjoy beers in between.

At the end of his first cross-country season at Queen's, John was convinced by a teammate and senior athlete, Rob Auld, to give the beer mile a try. A few guys who had been on the team for a number of years would get the interested runners together, decide on a date, and make it happen.

That year, the men from Queen's had discussed the beer mile with local athletes at a cross-country meet at Lehigh University in Pennsylvania, who thought it was the coolest thing and wanted to give it a try. It was then that Markell and company decided there needed to be a "standard" set of rules if people were going to compare times from events held in different cities. One fall night in 1993, the group met at 107 York Street in Kingston, the home city of Queen's University. They decided on the following rules:

- Cans only. (Glass bottles were not allowed on university grounds.)
- They wanted the beer to be "Canadian," so 5 percent alcohol by volume (ABV) was required. (Most beers in the United States were lighter at the time, and the Canadians wouldn't stand for it. The 355 mL size made sense as that was the size of almost all cans.)
- Beers were to be grabbed off the track by the runner; no assistance of a table or spectator.
- The cans had to be opened by each runner as they

came into the zone and had to remain unaltered. This meant no tampering with the can in any way to allow for quicker drinking (i.e., no shotgunning).

- To cover the full distance of a mile (1,609 meters), runners are given a nine-meter "chug-zone" to finish their beer.

Before starting the lap, the runner must turn their beer upside down over their head to prove it is finished. At the end of the race, if the runner looked like they just showered in beer, it was clear they didn't finish their beer.

The rules were written down on a piece of lined paper, and that was it. The rules of the beer mile, soon to be known as the "Kingston Rules," were official. In the end, it was all based on an honor system. The group wanted a level playing field across the world, no matter where the beer mile was run. This was the underground era of the beer mile. Once a year, when the cross-country season ended, runners would sneak onto the local track after the sun went down to put it all on the line. The grand prize: bragging rights until the next year. This was well before the time of videotaping time trials, online critics, and viral mass media; that all followed years later.

The hero of the early races at Queen's was Dan Michaluk, the strongest drinker of the group. His incredible ability to drink every beer in ten seconds or less allowed him to win most of the races by over a minute, consistently posting times in the 5:40s. However, the growing popularity of the event, from a participation and spectator standpoint, wasn't primarily to come watch these guys run fast. It had to do with the amusement of watching people fail. And by fail, I mean vomit. A lot. Mark "Spinorama" Arsenault became a legend for a move where he would spin a complete 360 degrees while vomiting the entire rotation. Every single beer mile. Spinorama. His stomach was more volatile than Donald Trump with the media.

Collegiate folklore tells us that from the early 1990s to late 2000s, the beer mile slowly gained steam with runners across Canada, from British Columbia to Prince Edward Island. Races were run on local tracks, after dark, and if you were to look from a distance, you would just think it was a late-night running club doing some intervals after a long day of work. That couldn't be further from the truth. Runners by the dozen would meet on a semi-annual, sometimes even seasonal, basis to compete for bragging rights in the four-beer, four-lap showdown. In the late 1990s, beermile.com was established to serve as an online database for beer mile results. Patrick Butler, a young beer mile enthusiast, would compile all the results sent his way, so that individuals could see how they ranked against the best in the world. He single-handedly dragged the underground event onto the global stage, allowing ordinary beer milers across the globe to share their results. The Kingston rules were listed on the website so everyone knew the criteria for a legitimate race. Once the website gained traction, it advanced to have an "official" list where users could submit a video with their entry. The videos would be reviewed on a case-by-case basis to see if the participants followed the rules before deciding if the race would be counted as official or not. Technology and social media allowed the event rooted in the twentieth century to evolve, as now even the average Joe could upload a video and get on the list. In a growing environment of obscure world challenges like running a marathon while juggling, or fastest 5K while wearing a full suit, the beer mile fit right in. Over time, Butler tweaked the rules listed on beermile.com to accommodate for the evolving sport. The website currently lists the following:

All official standard races need to adhere to all of the below.

1. Each competitor drinks four cans of beer and runs four laps, ideally on a track (start, beer, then lap, then beer, then lap, then beer, then lap, then beer, then lap, finish).
2. Beer must be consumed before the lap is begun, within the transition area which is the 10-meter zone before the start/finish line on a 400-meter track.
3. The race begins with the drinking of the first beer in the last meter of the transition zone to ensure the competitors run a complete mile (1,609 meters).
4. Women also drink four beers in four laps (past rule lists only required ladies to drink three beers).
5. Competitors must drink canned beer, and the cans should not be less than 355 mL (the standard can volume) or 12 ounces (the imperial equivalent). Bottles may be substituted for cans as long as they are at least 12 ounces (355 mL) in volume.
6. No specialized cans or bottles may be used that give an advantage by allowing the beer to pour at a faster rate. (i.e., "super mega mouth cans" or "wide mouth bottles" are prohibited.)
7. Beer cans must not be tampered with in any manner: i.e., no shotgunning or puncturing of the can except for opening the can by the tab at the top. The same applies to bottles—no straws or other aids are allowed in order to aid in the speed of pouring.
8. Beer must be a minimum of 5 percent alcohol by volume. Hard ciders and lemonades will not suffice. The

beer must be a fermented alcoholic beverage brewed from malted cereal grains and flavored with hops.

9. Each beer can must not be opened until the competitor enters the transition zone on each lap.
10. Competitors who vomit before they finish the race must complete one penalty lap at the end of the race (immediately after the completion of their fourth lap). Note: Vomiting more than once during the race still requires only one penalty lap at the end.

*It is strongly recommended, when attempting official records, to tip the empty beer can or bottle over your head at the end of a chug to verify an empty vessel.

In elite races, empty beers are collected, and the leftover is measured. A total of four ounces is allowed; anything over that results in disqualification.

Like pouring a perfect pint, the rules for the beer mile took time to settle down. Human achievement has been captured more easily on many occasions. Throughout history, many challenges have seemed impossible, but drive and determination have allowed individuals to achieve what many doubted. When Sir Edmund Hillary was the first man to climb Mount Everest, the challenge was clear and the achievement obvious as he stood atop the peak. The same went for Neil Armstrong when he was the first man to step foot on the moon.

Of course, it's Roger Bannister's famous four-minute mile that has inspired every runner since to achieve their personal best, and his story, oddly enough, draws a unique parallel to the evolution of the beer mile. So let's back up a bit.

In the 1940s, the world record for the mile had hit 4:01, where it came to a standstill. Medical professionals and scientists claimed it was physically impossible to break four minutes. More than just difficult or dangerous, physicians told athletes they would die before they ran four laps in under four minutes. This all changed just over a decade later.

Bannister was raised in a working-class family, and he used his talent for distance running to score a track scholarship to Oxford University where he studied medicine. He was an extraordinary athlete but decided to pass on competing in the 1948 Olympics. However, watching it sparked a fire inside Bannister, who set his sights on training for the 1952 Olympics. Four years later, he toed the line in the Olympic 1500 meter final, finishing a heartbreaking fourth. He contemplated quitting for months; he'd trained so hard but didn't even come home with a medal. In the end, his drive to prove to everyone, including himself, that he could do better kept him in the sport. This decision would change the history of the mile forever.

Fast forward to 1954, where the mile world record still sat at 4:01. Bannister kicked his training into overdrive, adding intense speed workouts and recruiting pacers to help him run faster. He knew he was knocking on the door of the first ever sub-four minute mile, but he wasn't the only one. Plenty of men were trying across the world, with his main rival being Australian John Landy. Every man knew if they were the first to do it, they would go down as a legend in track and field history.

While many believed it was impossible, scientists claimed that if it were to happen, conditions would have to be perfect. Not too hot, not too cold. Dry conditions. A nice, hard track. Tens of thousands of fans cheering to give the athlete that extra push. That was not the case on May 6, 1954. Despite cold temperatures and a soaked track, Bannister toed the line anyway. Six men started the race, two of them helping set the pace. By one lap to go, there was just Bannister and one of his pacers, Christopher Chataway, hitting the bell at 3:00. They needed a 59-second final lap to do it. In the final straightaway, Bannister pulled away from Chataway and leaned with everything he had at the line, collapsing in exhaustion. All he heard was the eruption of the crowd. 3:59.4! He had done it! He had broken the world record and broken the four-minute mile, something so many people told him he would kill himself trying to do. He had made history.

Over the next decade, plenty of athletes broke the four-minute mark after they realized that it was possible. Once Bannister had accomplished the impossible, suddenly dozens of elites could do it. This not only inspired middle distance runners but anyone who heard of the feat: once you stop believing something is impossible, it becomes possible.

The beer mile version of this was the race to run sub-five. Run a mile and drink four beers in under five minutes? No way. It wasn't until 2012 that the barrier seemed breakable. At the time, Canadian Jim Finlayson's world record of 5:09 had stood strong for five years. It was a complete anomaly, with the next closest times barely under six minutes. That stood true until 2012, when Josh Harris entered the scene.

While the rules were written in Canada, elite beer miling emerged across the world in Australia. In 2009, Harris, an Australian long distance runner from Launceston, Tasmania, attempted his first beer mile, finishing in 8:22. A last-minute invite to an event that featured the beer mile led to one of the most fun races of his life. He was instantly hooked. Shortly thereafter, he stumbled upon beermile.com and started scheming how he could run it faster and maybe one day get the Australian record, which sat at 6:14. When he discovered that the world record at the time was 5:09, he was shocked. How was that physically possible? Harris wanted to find out. He began researching; even if he could just find split times, it would help him understand how Finlayson could do it minutes quicker. He couldn't find splits, but by the end of the year, Harris had figured out how to get his chug time down to ten seconds out of a bottle, much better than the thirty seconds he started with previously.

In 2010, Harris won his club's annual beer mile in 6:33, becoming the second fastest Australian of all time. His running was great; it was the beers that were slowing him down. The only thing between him and the Australian record were the last three beers, which he averaged thirty-five seconds or so each to get them down. It wasn't until September that Harris would give the record another chance. After months of training, and lots of work on those latter beers, he managed to run 6:03 to officially become the Australian record holder. At this point, he was satisfied with his beer mile career. Finlayson's world record was so far out of reach that he was content with his Australian record. He still attended beer miles, but he would just show up to win, even running in jeans sometimes to show off.

Harris wasn't a beer miler by trade but rather an elite athlete who did the beer mile on the side. In 2012, he was selected to run for Australia at the World University Cross Country Championships in Łódź, Poland. With the annual beer mile being two days before leaving, he arrived at the race with no beers in hand. This didn't mean he wasn't racing, though. Harris showed up with a jug of chocolate milk, instead, as he was too competitive to give the race a total pass. (The chocolate milk mile follows the exact same rules as the beer mile—just replace the four beers with four cups of chocolate milk.) However, the highlight of this race wasn't to be his. Although he ran 4:58 for an Australian record in the chocolate milk mile, the most memorable performance of the day was run by James Hansen. He finished shortly after Harris in 5:23, hands over his head in celebration, as he had just annihilated Harris's Australian record for the beer mile. For the first time, Finlayson's 5:09 was within reach. Although it wouldn't be ratified as he used 4.6 percent ABV beers, it was a milestone in beer mile history.

After witnessing Hansen run so fast, Harris knew he should be able to cut a big chunk of time off his run if he could just get the chugs right. He planned on using a helpful tip he learned at a party since his last beer mile, which focused more on opening the throat rather than swallowing the beer. One week after Harris returned from Poland, the two Aussies had a beer mile showdown planned: former versus current Australian record holder. Yet again, the record went down when Harris crossed the line in 5:16, while Hansen struggled on beer four and had to run a penalty lap. Harris was excited as this race served as a warm-up race for him with the annual "Melbourne Autumn Classic" beer mile the next day.

On the start line, Harris knew the world record was within reach, and his run proved so. The Autumn Classic gathered a big crowd, and when he hit halfway at 2:34, Harris knew that it was his day. Crossing the line in 5:02 to the cheering crowd, Harris was on top of the world. He was so excited that he uploaded his race video online as soon as he got home, and it instantly went viral. What happened next would soon become a trend within the beer mile community. People across the world began criticizing the run. Some said Harris didn't tip the empty bottles over his head, while others argued there was too much foam left in the bottles. Up until this point, the beer mile was still "underground," and while there were "rules" on beermile.com, there were no official rules for leftover volume yet. After crossing the line in complete elation, Harris would end up disappointed as the run was not ratified.

One of Harris's main critics online is our third key player in the evolution of the beer mile, Corey Gallagher. At the time, the Canadian from Winnipeg, Manitoba, was the only other person in the world that was obviously trying to be the first man under five minutes in the beer mile. Similar to Harris, Gallagher typically ran one or two beer miles per year with his local running group. He had been consistently improving every year, from 12:58 in 2006, to 5:23 in early 2012.

After Harris's unofficial 5:02 video hit the internet, it was only a matter of time before someone would eclipse the five minute mark. Gallagher would go on to run 5:10 in August of the same year, coming agonizingly close to Finlayson's 5:09 world record that was clearly in serious danger. By this point, the beer mile was getting enough international attention that after the 2012 London Olympics, 800-meter runner Nick Symmonds even gave the beer mile a try. Coming off a fifth-place finish in the Olympic final, he ran an impressive 5:19. As it had done for so long, Finlayson's world record survived into another year. But this would be the final time.

If you have ever seen a professional beer mile, you will notice that over half of the field will wear a glove on their non-drinking hand. They aren't about to go plant tulips, or sprint 30 yards to catch a game-winning touchdown. Occasionally, a beer with a twist-off cap doesn't come off properly, but never had it caused an individual as much grief as it did to Josh Harris in April 2013. At the Melbourne Autumn Classic beer mile, once again Harris was toeing the line, looking for a fast but clean run. He had raced a cross-country race in the morning but wasn't too concerned; he knew he was fit enough to double back for the world record. Early on, it seemed to be the perfect run, hitting 72 after lap one, 2:30 after lap two, and 3:45 after lap three. He knew he was about to officially take down the world record and be the first man to go sub-five, when disaster hit. His last bottle cap wouldn't twist off! Ten seconds and a bloody hand later, he was able to chug the beer and start the lap at 4:06. Closing in an impressive 58 seconds, Harris broke the world record with his final time of 5:04. The run was clean as a whistle and got approved instantly on beermile.com. At the time, Harris was slightly disappointed because if it weren't for that bottle cap, he would have broken five minutes, but he wasn't too upset as he knew he was ready and there was no imminent threat.

That evening, James Hansen demanded another beer mile showdown. It would go down a few weeks later, and they would go on to call it "the sub-five attempt." The name lived up to expectations, as on May 4, 2013, Hansen went on to run 4:54.3, the first man to ever cross the line in under five minutes. Harris struggled on beer four and needed to run a penalty lap. Unfortunately, upon video review, Hansen's drinking was too messy to ratify. The rest of 2013 was quiet on the beer mile front, as Harris prepared for his debut in the marathon and Hansen was trying to make it as a professional 1500-meter runner. They both figured it was just a matter of time before one of them became the first ever to officially break five.

Both Harris and Hansen were blindsided on April 28, 2014, to see that James Nielsen, a man they had never heard of before, had run 4:57. Nielsen knew all the details. He knew the date of the Melbourne race, he knew the anniversary of the first sub-four minute mile was approaching, and he knew if he didn't break five, then no one would ever see his attempt. By this point, a reporter from *Outside* magazine was flying all the way from the US to come watch Harris prepare for the Melbourne Autumn Classic. The reporter was halfway to Australia when Nielsen released his video to the world.

This race would forever be a milestone in beer mile history and would turn the sport into a viral online sensation.

In the video, James Nielsen heads to the track at the College of Marin in Northern California with his wife, who's filming. He tells the camera he is in about 4:10 mile shape, not as fit as he was in college, but hopefully more than fit enough for this challenge. Nielsen has been quietly training for this day for a long time, hoping to be the first man to ever break five minutes.

He explains to the camera how much training he has put into this world-record/sub-five attempt. He used the training strategies of professional hot dog eaters in order to expand his stomach. This included eating an entire watermelon in one sitting, as quickly as possible. Doing this could only help his stomach deal with all the carbon dioxide he was about to put into it, right? Nielsen also studied the anatomy of the esophagus to make sure he maximized the amount of volume he could consume in the shortest amount of time possible. He says to the camera, "I can drink a beer in about two to three seconds out of a glass, I can pour it out of a can in about eight. I need to be somewhere between; I need to be able to drink that beer in about four or five, maybe six seconds. I can do that, I have done it. I need to do it four times in a row." He claims he consulted with "some of the best chemical minds on the planet" to understand the composition of beer and the carbon dioxide displacement within the can. They have told him he needs it to be at an optimal temperature in order to get as much carbon dioxide to exit the beer as possible when he opens it.

Shortly after arriving at the track, Nielsen warms up and sets the stage. Four cans of Budweiser, meeting the 355 mL/12 ounce and 5 percent ABV requirements, are set up on a table nine meters back of the finish line. This nine-meter "chug zone" was soon to be viewed by millions worldwide. With camera in hand, his wife gives James the starting commands, "On your mark, get set . . . Go!" He had secretly put dozens of hours of training in for this moment. Stomach expansion, studying fluid dynamics, throat anatomy. He wasn't joking around, and this was his chance to be the first man to break five minutes in the beer mile. He cracks open his room temperature Budweiser, tilts his head back 45 degrees, and finishes the first beer in about five seconds, before throwing it in a trash can and sprinting off. Through studying "the science of the beer mile," he knew warm beer would be less carbonated and easier on the stomach.

Through experimenting, he found that the quickest way for him to drink a beer was to seal his lips to the can, tilt back to 45 degrees and suck it out. He claimed this allowed him to drink each beer about three seconds faster than by simply pouring it out. This was one of the main arguments in the controversy to come. He comes into the chug zone at seventy seconds, well ahead of five minute pace. He grabs his second beer and sucks the beer out in under four seconds, pours it upside down over his head to show it's empty, then takes off running again. He comes into beer number three at 2:26, and makes quick work of it as well. Running into his fourth and final beer, you can hear Nielsen breathing harder than before, panting and taking a couple of seconds before opening the beer. He is at 3:45 and needs a big final lap if he wants to break the five minute barrier. Luckily, his training came in when he needed it most, running a 63 for the last 400 meters. 4:57! He had done what no man had done before and what soon would be seen by millions. The only words he had after he crossed the line was, "That is really painful."

Nielsen's world record caught traction with over one million views on YouTube within the first forty-eight hours. Soon after, the run was picked up by *The Wall Street Journal*, *USA Today*, and *Sports Illustrated*. All of a sudden, it wasn't just collegiate distance runners that were interested in the beer mile, but average Joes across the world.

As expected, since Nielsen was on a track alone, with only his wife filming, people immediately questioned if the run were real. On a Canadian running site, Trackie.ca, comments poured in from viewers like, "So right off the bat he ruined the legitimacy by not presenting the can upside down over his head," and "The big idiot didn't turn the first one over." Some even accused him of tampering with the beers and replacing the volume with water. To this Nielsen replied, "Replacing beer with water? Right, like I'd infiltrated Budweiser and tampered with the exact cans I'd end up buying," in one interview. As for not turning the first can over his head, Nielsen claimed to forget, which is understandable with the craziness of the first beer, and when every millisecond counts. Beermile. com states that overturning the empty vessel over your head is "recommended" but is not required, so the run was able to be approved. The final argument concerns the fact he claims to "suck the beer out" of the cans. Yes, this was hypothetically possible for beer one, but how could he possibly deeply inhale for four to five seconds on the other three while panting heavily due to oxygen debt? This issue was never addressed.

Legitimate or not, there is no denying that Nielsen

breaking the five minute barrier brought the beer mile into the public eye. Shortly after, FloTrack decided that it was time to determine who the best in the world really was. No more solo time trials on a track. No more hiding behind keyboards across the world from one another, claiming to be the best. The top ten in the world (as listed on beermile.com) would be invited to Austin, Texas, to race head-to-head. The winner would take home all the bragging rights, as well as upwards of $5,000. Because of FloTrack's reach, this beer mile would be heard about and seen by every serious running fan in North America, and the date for the big showdown was December 3, 2014. This is where my beer mile story begins.

CHAPTER THREE

# So You Want to Run a Beer Mile?

It's December 17, 2016. Elvira Montes toes the start line at the Beer Mile World Championships. She is back for her third year in a row and looking to run faster than ever before. While the crowd didn't necessarily show up just to watch her race, she has no doubt she will impress them once again. And no, that isn't because she's looking to break any records. It's because she's eighty-two years old.

She doesn't have much speed, but her running is steady. She has no problem putting back four beers and running a mile. She runs down the final straightaway waving to the crowd and giving a few fans high-fives. She put her children, her grandchildren, and dozens of other competitors to shame, crossing the line in 20:47.

The next time you say the beer mile is hard, think about what Elvira, or your granny, would say.

If you're not sure where to start, have no fear. This chapter is targeted at the beginner—someone who's brand new to the beer mile, or has only run one or two. Here I will introduce how the recreational runner can get involved without being too intimidated and lay out a few basic tips and tricks; the do's and the don'ts of the beer mile. This is for those who really just want to leave that pesky friend you can't seem to beat in a 5K in the dust. Or maybe you just need a pointer or two to make sure you get around the track without throwing up. This chapter is for you.

The first and most important rule of the beer mile is that you are of legal drinking age and have transportation arrangements to and from the venue that don't involve you driving or using any sort of machinery. Remember that the beer mile is entertaining to watch, so I can almost guarantee a family member or friend would drive you to and from the track. Remember that ultimately, you are doing this for fun, but as with any fun activity, safety and responsibility are the first orders of business. Run responsibly.

Secondly, you want to eat smart on race day and the few days leading up to it. Keep it simple with things you know digest well, and make sure to eat several hours in advance of the race. My rule of thumb: if you can imagine it coming back up, avoid it. That means avoiding big meals and heavier foods and keeping it simple with easy-to-digest carbs, like bread and bagels. Yes, that means that Five Guys double cheeseburger will have to wait until after the race. Within five hours of a beer mile, you'll never find me eating anything but bread and Nutella.

In terms of timing your last meal, you know your own body best, but I'd say make sure you eat at the very least two and a half hours before race time.

Important note: Beer miling on a completely empty stomach is just as bad, if not worse, than eating a meal fifteen minutes before the race. If you haven't eaten all day, your stomach hasn't had to stretch/expand all day and won't cope well with the carbonation and volume you're about to give it. Make sure you eat enough on race day. Otherwise, the result won't be pretty. If you want testimony, I know a few people that can speak from personal experience.

For a sponsored race, the beers will be provided and set up for you. However, if you are bringing your own beer, make sure they are secured! We are trying to make this as easy and smooth as possible, and foam is your biggest enemy. If the beer has been turbulent, you just punched a one-way ticket to foam city.

Now, for the running. My general advice to you in this regard is quite simple: break down each lap into three sections, as follows.

### 1. The first hundred meters

After you finish your beer, don't worry about how fast you run the first one hundred meters. Just focus on one thing. Burping. Get every possible ounce of carbonation out. Everyone thinks they struggle because of the volume, but that's usually not the issue; for most people, it's the carbonation that's the killer. The next beer doesn't go down well if your stomach is filled with gas, so make sure to burp!

### 2. The middle two hundred meters

By the time you've rounded the first bend, all the carbonation you're going to get up is out, so it's time to pick up the pace. For the first two laps, I'd say aim for a bit faster than your 5K pace when running the middle section of the lap. You want to feel in control, and it's easier to pick it up later on in the race than to go out too hard then crash and burn.

### 3. The final hundred meters

As you turn onto the home straightaway, you'll want to ease off the pace. The most important part of every lap is the final nine meters: the chug zone. Easing off the pace allows you to go into the zone smooth and relaxed. This is where you will crush the competition. In the chug zone, almost all inexperienced beer milers will run all the way up to their beer, open it in a rush, take half a sip, and need to take a break to breathe. Then they'll spend the next minute making about a dozen awful attempts at finishing their beer. It's a great strategy if you want to make the race harder than it already is.

Instead, slow down and relax. Open your beer to let the carbonation out, but don't be in an immediate rush to start drinking it. Remember that carbonation is your enemy, so give it time to go into the air instead of into your stomach. Once you feel ready, start drinking. Your goal should be to get at least half the beer down in that first chug. Get out a good burp and don't try to chug again until you think you can get at least a quarter of the beer down. This calm and composed strategy will beat the rushed, out-of-breath panicking of your competition.

Repeat three more times, and you're done. It's as simple as that! Well, not quite. As mentioned earlier, it is better to be conservative for the first half of the race. If you finish your third beer and are feeling great (very unlikely, but if you are, good for you!), start to pick up the pace on lap three.

Lap four is not one you can plan for. In my first beer mile, I ran the entire last lap with my neck cranked to the sky, moving at a snail's pace, barely able to hold down the beer. However using the tips mentioned here, as well as some other pointers that I'll expand on later, it has gotten much easier.

The point is, you'll have to see how you feel going into the final lap before determining a strategy. If you feel good, I recommend getting gradually faster every hundred meters, and when you turn into the home stretch, remember there is no beer waiting for you! Bring it home with all you've got.

With that in mind, once you have run a few beer miles and feel comfortable, I challenge you to attempt the 1-2-3-4. Drink the first beer in one chug. Second beer in two chugs. Third in three. Fourth in four. The first time I tried this, I cut thirty seconds off my total chug time, bringing my overall time from 6:22 to 5:52.

Disclaimer: Later in the race, don't trust the burp. The carbonation usually comes out a lot easier on laps one and two, but as the race goes on, you have to be more careful to differentiate between what is a burp and what is a puke (and a fun penalty lap). If you do have to throw up, it is courtesy to pull off to the side of the track or race course for two reasons. First, while it can be entertaining to watch, nobody wants to get puked on. If there is a garbage can close by, use it! Secondly, if another competitor isn't feeling great and sees you throw up, that will probably be the straw that breaks the camel's back, and soon there will be a dozen of you throwing up together. If it does happen to you, you will feel a lot better after you've run your penalty lap with pride, as many a beer miler has done before you.

CHAPTER FOUR

# So You Want to Win a Beer Mile?

CONGRATS! YOU'VE MADE it past your first few beer miles, and now, it isn't just about finishing. No, you want to cross the line first and have all the bragging rights. After this chapter, you will have all the tools you need to not only win your race but also challenge the best in the world.

The winner of a beer mile is not necessarily the fittest individual, or the one who drinks the most; instead, it's the person who can handle the combination of the two the best. I'm going to take you through the four keys to the beer mile: drinking technique, stomach expansion, beer intervals, and race day strategy.

Before you get started, you need a basic level of fitness. The best beer milers are elite runners who drink, not elite drinkers who run. By no means do you need to be an Olympic-caliber athlete or consistently winning track or road races, but having consistent weekly mileage under your belt will go a long way on race day.

## DRINKING TECHNIQUE

Although you don't necessarily need to be the quickest miler of the bunch to win, you definitely need to be fit enough to stay within contention on the run laps. Where the race is won or lost is the chug zone. It is crucial that the nine-meter stretch where you have to drink your beer is the strongest part of your race. Here is where you'll witness your competitors struggling to catch their breath, finish their beers, and potentially throw up. For the context of this chapter, if you throw up, you've already lost the race.

If you're new to the beer mile and haven't run many before, I suggest using cans. The beer will flow a little slower, and the can is much more conducive to taking breaks mid-beer. Bottles tend to aggressively foam up if you suddenly take the beer away from your mouth, and that is the last thing you need. Once you know you can handle the speed of a can, make the transition to bottles.

Now we can get into the science of the beer mile. Regardless of your vessel of choice (can or bottle), the key is to get maximum airflow. It comes down to fluid dynamics: the more air you allow into the bottle or can, the quicker the beer will flow as the air is pushing it out. Of course, this isn't something any of us were taught in school, so in the name of "science," I did some experimenting.

In the fall of 2014, I was finally back on my feet after two weeks off running because of a knee injury. It was a Friday night, and I knew I was going to be giving the beer mile a try the next day. I asked my roommate and engineer, Greg Smith, his opinion on the quickest way to drink beer out of a can. He replied, "There is only one way to find out," as he slapped a six-pack of Old Milwaukee down on the counter. Greg has been my beer mile coach ever since.

Most people tend to think that in order to drink the beer as quickly as possible, you need to have the beer vertical. But, if you follow these few tips I learned, you will fly by them in the transition zone:

1. Have as little contact with the vessel as possible. The less contact you have with the can or bottle, the better. If your top and bottom lips are in contact with the vessel, less air is able to flow into it, slowing down the speed of your chug. Try a practice chug with water. First, try with both lips making contact, then try an attempt with your top lip off and only your bottom lip making contact. You will immediately notice the difference.

2. Find your perfect angle. While I wish I could suggest an optimal angle for flow, I've found that it is highly dependent on the individual. You will probably hear 45 degrees is best, and I recommend trying that first. Then try an angle closer to vertical, as well as an angle closer to horizontal. I have seen beer chugged super-fast at all sorts of angles, so you really need to find what angle works best for you. Practice makes perfect.

3. Take big gulps. If you are swallowing too often, the beer has nowhere to go! Try taking as few gulps as possible. This will obviously range based on how big your mouth is, but I can usually get a beer down in three to four big gulps. Wait until the beer is almost overflowing your mouth before swallowing. Once again, practice makes perfect.

4. Track your speed. This is where it gets fun. If you have family and friends also interested in the beer mile, you can create a leaderboard listing your chug personal bests/records. The goal is to progress and be able to get it down (whether water, non- alcoholic beer, or beer) as quickly as you possibly can. By keeping track, you can measure up against your friends and see if you are getting faster.

## STOMACH EXPANSION

The most common aspect of the beer mile that people have an issue with is stomach discomfort. Your body is not used to being filled with forty-eight ounces of beer in such a short time frame, so here are a few tips to make race day as comfortable as possible. (These are techniques used by professional eaters, just a lot less intense and fine-tuned for the beer mile. Thankfully, four beers are a lot easier to get down than dozens of hotdogs or hamburgers.)

1. Eat a few BIG meals in the days leading up to the race. A day or two before, try eating until you can't eat anymore. You should feel like you do at the end of an all-you-can-eat-buffet, where you literally can't eat another bite.

2. Important note: Do NOT do this in your last meal in the hours leading up to the race. While it will stretch out your stomach, the food will not have time to digest, and you'll likely see it come back up mid-race.

3. A favorite pre-race food of mine is watermelon, mostly because watermelon is delicious, but it's also easy to eat quite a bit of it, and it is very water dense (92 percent), so you get a good result as it is digested.

4. Another option is to eat as you regularly would, and follow it up with one or two bottle chugs. This is a great simulation of beers three and four when your stomach is already full and you've got to struggle a bit put them back. As mentioned above, you can fill an empty can/bottle up with water, or use a non-alcoholic beer to allow for practice on work nights, sans hangover the next morning.

5. You don't need to be doing this weeks out from your beer mile, just once or twice in the days leading up to it. On race day, try to stick to foods you know will keep your stomach happy. For me, this means avoiding heavy meals like rice and pasta and sticking to simple, easy-to-digest bread products.

## BEER INTERVALS

As mentioned earlier, if you're looking to win a beer mile and run a fast time, you need to be in good running shape. Depending on your regular racing distance(s), your training week will look a lot different. Regardless, I want to run you through a beer mile specific workout.

A classic track workout consists of 400-meter (quarter-mile) repeats. Completing between eight and sixteen reps can be a great way to get the legs moving, whether the goal race is a mile or a marathon. To adjust this for beer mile training, you can complete the same workout, but as you go into an interval or two, chug a beer either before or after. This will simulate chugging a beer while out of breath and running with beer in your stomach. You want to try this out towards the end of the workout, because if it goes poorly, at least you're almost done. Here is how I would suggest doing it:

## 8 x 400m Beer Mile Workout

4* x 400m at race pace** (2 minutes rest)
1 x 400m with beer chug before repeat (2 minutes rest)
2 x 400m finishing with a beer chug (2 minutes rest)
1 x 400m

*You can adjust the amount of 400s before or after the chug laps depending on your fitness level.

**Race pace will depend on how many reps you are doing. If you are only doing eight intervals, you should be very close to goal beer mile race pace, which will be between your mile and two-mile personal best pace. If you are doing upwards of sixteen intervals, start at 10K race pace and with each repeat, get quicker so you are finishing at goal beer mile pace.

## RACE DAY STRATEGY

Now that you've got the fitness, the drinking technique, and the stomach ready to go, all that remains are race-day tactics. My best advice: keep it simple. The key is to not go out too hard—if you are out of breath, you will have to take multiple breaks mid-beer and lose precious time in the transition zone. I always try to have my first lap be my slowest, getting faster and faster with each quarter mile. This guarantees you will have smooth transition zones and still allows you to hammer the last quarter if you have a lot left in the tank. You'll be glad you paced yourself when you fly by your competitors.

Based on your practice (and if you have done previous beer miles), you should set goals. If you want to get really serious about it, delegate a friend as a "coach," and get them to take your splits. Beer mile splits are usually taken as follows: Beer 1, Lap 1, Beer 2, Lap 2, Beer 3, Lap 3, Beer 4, Lap 4.

Then, after you finish, you can see what went well and where to improve (this is usually beers 3 and 4), then go back to the drawing board to plan your next race splits.

I sent my friends my goal splits on Snapchat right before I broke the world record (photo of that can be found in this book's insert), and below is a sample split chart for you to fill in yourself. Good luck!

|  | Beer 1/ Lap 1 | Beer 2/ Lap 2 | Beer 3/ Lap 3 | Beer 4/ Lap 4 | Total Time |
|---|---|---|---|---|---|
| Previous Beer Mile (if any) |  |  |  |  |  |
| Goal Beer Mile |  |  |  |  |  |

# CHAPTER FIVE

# Having a Support Team

I HAD PULLED up Dad in my phone contacts a dozen times in the past week, my finger millimeters from pushing the FaceTime icon, just to lock my phone and put it down. I had no idea how I was going to do it.

I had already told my older brother, Jordan, all about the beer mile. Chugging beers, running laps, and how I was about to fly thousands of miles to do both against the best in the world. He was just as excited as I was. Unfortunately, rehearsing with him did nothing to help me when I was face to face with my mom and dad . . . obviously, this was going to take a bit of explaining. And oh boy, would it ever.

Finally, so nervous I felt that my heart was going to beat out of my chest, I called them.

"Hi, Dad. How's it going?"

"Good. Diane, hurry up. Lewis is online! How's studying going? Your exams are coming up soon, right?"

I would be racing two days before my first of five exams. And to be honest, I'd not only forgotten about the exams altogether, but also all the hours required to study for them. Great, I'd already dug myself a hole.

"Oh yeah . . . exams. I'll be ready for those." And I would, but I had an ulterior motive for the call. "Remember I had that 3K time trial to make the indoor track team the other day? I managed to run 8:50! A twenty-five-second personal best to finish third."

"Wow, that's amazing, Lewis!" Mom poked her head into the frame with a smile.

"You must be really pleased," Dad nodded, "you are running really well so soon after your injury!" This was true; I was only back on my feet in the past week after being sidelined for close to a month with some left knee pain.

"Yes . . . and Dad . . ."

"Yes?"

"You've heard of the beer mile, right?"

"No."

I was so afraid of how he would respond to what I said next, but I was committed at this point.

"Well, it's just a like a regular mile . . . but you drink a beer before every lap." Before they could ask any questions, I took a quick breath, then the rest came out in a rush. "I ran the fastest time ever in Ontario a few weeks ago and became the third fastest ever in Canadian history. I've been invited to the World Championships in Austin, Texas, and I have already booked my flights down leaving on December 2, racing on the third, and getting back on the fourth."

It was so silent you could hear a pin drop. I cringed as I waited; how was he going to respond?

"What the hell? Where? What? How is that possible? Is that healthy? What about your exams? They have guns in Texas! What about your exams?"

"I can get back in time, my first exam is two days after the race."

"Okay," he replied in a monotone, unexcited voice. "Okay Lewis. Diane, over to you." He left the frame and sat elsewhere to process what I had just told him while I filled my mom in on how I got into the beer mile in the first place.

I had first heard of the beer mile earlier that year, but by no means could I explain it well at that time. I knew it involved running four laps of the track and chugging four beers as quickly as you could, but that's about it. I hadn't given the event a second thought until my university's team was invited to a nearby university for that team's annual beer mile during the off-season. It sounded like a good time. I thought, *Could it really be that hard?* I would go on to find out just how challenging it was, placing fifth and running well over six minutes in my first attempt at the chugging and running event. It was an absolute frenzy of panting, burping, and sprinting. It was way more fun than it sounds.

As much fun as it was, the beer mile remained strictly an off-season spectacle, and the following week, I dove into training for the quickly approaching summer track season. I spent all of May living the life of an elite athlete while visiting family in Scotland and England. I would wake up and train, spend most of the day relaxing, then train again in the evening. I wasn't complaining.

It paid off as I would go on to run personal bests in every

event I competed in that summer, from the 800 meters all the way up to the 5K. It was the best summer of racing I had had to date.

That August of 2014, I was going into my third year of university, and having met my summer goal of running under four minutes in the 1500m, it was safe to say I was excited for the cross country season. The buildup was going well, as I ran personal bests at 6K and 8K in my first two races. However, the streak of consistent running came to a heartbreaking end when some nagging patellar tendinopathy took a turn for the worse in early October. I was ordered to shut down my season and spend two weeks in the pool, water running. At the time, it was extremely disappointing. However, looking back, the injury was a blessing in disguise.

If you have ever water run (also known as aqua jogging) before, you will understand why fourteen days in a row of it was a daunting task. It is one of the best forms of cross training as it allows you to get a good workout in while keeping your running muscles active without the impact that causes most running-related injuries. If you haven't seen it, imagine yourself with a massive flotation belt on, submerged neck deep in a pool, while imitating a running motion underwater. It feels awkward, looks ridiculous, and everyone else at the pool stares at you as if you are a psychopath, probably because you must have a few screws loose to do it, especially alone.

Once the fourteen-day sentence of complete boredom was up, my physiotherapist approved me to slowly start running again. While it was only a few slow, easy runs a week, it was an incredible escape from being in the pool. I started running again in the middle of October of that year, and while tryouts for the indoor track team were in four weeks, I figured

I wouldn't be in competitive shape until January with the lack of running and return from injury.

Luckily, injury recovery went well over the new few weeks. (I can't count the number of times throughout my career that I relied heavily on the support of my rehab team.) I was now able to go for full runs with the team. Autumn was in full effect, and for southwestern Ontario that meant the leaves were changing color rapidly. In September, the team would run trails, and apart from the odd root, it wasn't difficult footing by any means. However, by late October the leaves had changed from their usual green to a yellowish red and started to fall. In a couple of weeks, we wouldn't even be able to see the trail beneath our feet as it would be completely covered in leaves.

On my first run back, our pace was quicker than usual, probably because the number of days above freezing temperatures were numbered. We ran through the center of campus, where a majority of people stared at us, judging us by our split shorts that most wouldn't wear in the humid, hot days of summer, never mind late October. Halfway through our run, someone from the back of the pack asked the group if anyone had seen the latest FloTrack announcement. A few nodded in agreement that they had seen it, including me, while others had no idea what he was talking about. Earlier that day, FloTrack had announced they would be hosting the inaugural Beer Mile World Championships in Austin, Texas at the beginning of December. As members of a university track team, we had all tried a beer mile or two at some point, however, none of us were remotely close to being good enough to be invited to the World Championships. Therefore, we didn't think twice about the announcement.

The reminder of the race announcement had sparked my

curiosity, so when I got home after practice, I read through the full article on FloTrack's website. On December 3, a community track in Austin, Texas would host the best beer milers in the world, who would be racing head-to-head to crown a world champion. If you were ranked in the top ten in the world on beermile.com, FloTrack would provide flights and accommodation, in essence an all-expense paid trip. As I was browsing the details, one of my roommates, Greg Smith, came into the room and asked what I was looking at. At the time, I lived in a house of seven. There were two runners: Phil and me; as well as five other guys: Mike, Iain, Elliot, Greg, and Alex. They were all huge fans of any sort of competition and enjoyed coming to watch Phil and me race. They had all heard of the beer mile as Phil and I had raced our first one earlier that year, but Greg wanted a reminder of the exact rules. As I explained, the rest of the guys trickled into the room. As a group, we sat in the living room and watched race videos of the fastest guys in the world. *How could they drink so much beer and run so fast without puking?*

That Saturday, our house went to the local all-you-can-eat sushi restaurant for lunch, a monthly tradition for us. (Really, it was more like a weekly tradition.) Roughly 200 pieces of sushi later, Mike brought up the beer mile, and how he would love to see one live. I've always been a sucker for a challenge, so after a bit of peer pressure I agreed to run one that evening at 6 p.m. Just a few hours later, filled with regret and several pounds of seaweed, rice, and raw fish, my housemates and I walked over to the neighborhood track with four cans of Old Milwaukee. It would be my third ever beer mile; in April of that year, I debuted with a 6:11 while in great drinking shape and poor running shape, and in August, I had out-leaned Phil at the line for a 6:22 while in incredible running shape and awful drinking shape. Granted, drinking shape is a bit of an abstract term: typically, there is a direct relationship between the number of times you have enjoyed a few drinks recently and your drinking shape. As a result, during the off-season as a college athlete, you are in great drinking shape, while towards the end of a racing season (which includes very few nights out), you are in bad drinking shape. As I was in mid-season for this post-sushi beer mile, it is safe to say I wasn't in great drinking shape.

It was about 15 degrees Fahrenheit, and it started to lightly snow as we got to the track; fairly typical weather for London, Ontario in late October. In three layers of running clothes, I jogged a few laps of the track in order to warm up properly. The last thing I needed was another injury. Just for laughs, I had a pale green cape on that would immediately become part of my signature attire. (It was from our cross country training camp in August where we were split into teams for games, and every team had their own color of cape.) I had worn it in my first two beer miles, so why not wear it again? As the spectators—my roommates—were starting to lose feeling in their fingers, we decided it was go time. I felt like I was going to throw up an entire roll of spicy salmon, and I hadn't even started yet. *What was there to lose? Just my lunch, and maybe my dignity.*

I was the lone competitor on the start line. *No matter how poorly it went, at least I was going to win, right?* Greg got the stopwatch out on his phone to time the effort. I remember thinking to myself, *This is going to absolutely suck, but damn will it be some good entertainment.* The first beer went down relatively smooth, and off I ran, similar to as if I had just started a track interval. A lap of burping later, I grabbed my second beer. Just like the first, I had no trouble and made quick work of it.

However, the second lap was a different story. I could start to feel the beer sloshing around in my stomach. Grabbing beer three, I was out of breath, which caused all sorts of issues. Half way through the beer, I needed to take a break to breathe. After a second or two, I started drinking again and barely got anything down before I needed another break. It felt impossible! I needed to get the beer down, but holding my breath was not an option as I was gasping for air after running hard for 800 meters. I somehow finished up beer three and took off for the third lap. I made it through three beers and three laps in relatively good shape, but beer four was far from smooth. Five or six attempts and close to a minute later, I got it down and started my final lap. It took every piece of willpower I had to make it through that lap, with waves of nausea escalating every 100 meters. Crossing the line in 6:24, every piece of sushi I thought would have been digested by now came right back up. Wave after wave. Although not even close to the worlds' qualifying time of 5:30, at least I provided some quality entertainment for my friends.

We walked home laughing about how ridiculous the event was, wondering how it was even possible for someone to break five minutes. Within minutes of getting home, I showered and brushed my teeth to freshen up. I remember chugging a Gatorade and three glasses of water to replenish the fluids I just lost. I wasn't feeling the alcohol at all, probably because three of the four beers had come back up. I checked my phone to see a Facebook message from a teammate, Chris Balestrini, to our cross country group, "Western Triathlon Club is hosting their beer mile at Banting High School at 9 p.m., anyone want to join?" What were the odds? The same track I had just run on and thrown up all over, would see its second beer mile within hours. I laughed and asked my roommates if they wanted to go watch. Their consensus: We'll watch, but now that all the sushi is gone, do you think you can run faster?

Remember when I said I was a sucker for a challenge? As crazy as it may sound, I knew I could run faster. It was at that exact moment that Greg solidified his role as my beer mile coach. For the next ninety minutes, we watched videos of James Nielsen, Josh Harris, and Corey Gallagher running well under 5:15 and Greg noticed I wasn't running the actual mile much slower, it was the drinking that was slowing me down. He figured I could get down the first beer just as quick as they could, but by beer three and four, I was taking thirty to forty-five seconds, while they were finishing theirs in about ten. If I could somehow get those beers down quicker, I could break six minutes. By some miracle, the boys convinced me I could run faster in my second beer mile within three hours, so I grabbed four more cans of beer, threw on my cape, and off we went.

We walked over to the track at 8:45, and it was 10 degrees colder than earlier. It was pitch black, so we had to walk over half a lap of the track to find the group of roughly thirty triathletes half way through the back straight. Participants were dressed in ridiculous costumes from morphsuits to gorilla outfits. We quickly spotted my teammate, Chris, who was wearing nothing but his speedo. Such is the spirit of the beer mile. On top of the twenty-five or so people racing, there were another thirty or so watching, including half of the men's cross country team. They all made the trip out to see me attempt to break six minutes. Having my teammates come out to watch and support gave me more motivation to go for it.

Sporting a long-sleeved winter-grade running jacket, two pairs of full tights, a toque, and a winter mitt on my left hand, I was dressed for the occasion. My right hand needed to stay bare to open the beer; it was numb instantly. And of course, I had the green cape tied around my neck. Everyone was called to the line, and soon enough we were off, and I didn't know what to think. The first beer was my best chug of the day, but the first lap felt awful. The cold air stung my lungs, and my legs ached from the race just hours before. My teammate, Kevin Blackney, had the stopwatch going and I remember being at the halfway point, well under three minutes. *I was on pace*! Beer three and lap three went smoothly as well. Before I knew it, the fourth beer was down, and I heard, "4:44!" It wasn't a matter of whether or not I would break six minutes anymore, but by how much. I crossed the line ahead of the field with my frozen hands in the air. I had done it! The crowd cheered as Kevin announced the time: 5:52! In a matter of hours, I had shaved thirty seconds off my beer mile personal best and was within twenty seconds of a world championship qualifying time. Once everyone had finished, we had an awards ceremony. This wasn't the Olympics, where three athletes would stand on their post of the podium with millions of fans across the world watching while the winner's national anthem was played. It was so dark out that you couldn't see ten feet in front of you. Nevertheless, there wasn't a single person at the event who wasn't laughing or smiling about what they had just experienced. In a sense, this almost seemed like more fun. The rowdy group hushed down as the race organizers announced third and second place finishers. Everyone knew their names as they were part of the triathlon group. Then, from the middle of the huddle of three dozen people shivering in the cold, "And our winner for today, Capeman!" At that moment, my nickname was born. I walked to the middle of the group and gave a quick wave, before being handed a $15 gift card to BeerTown, a local restaurant! *Wow, I had just won a prize for winning a beer mile.* I had a strange feeling this was just the beginning of something special.

The next day, I went to the library with the intention of studying for an upcoming exam, but couldn't get my mind off the events of the night before, so I pulled up the information on the FloTrack World Championships on my laptop. I knew the world's best men and women would be assembling in Austin, but the question was: Would I be one of them, or just another person tuned in live?

At this time, the beer mile was rapidly gaining momentum. The event was going viral within the running community; nothing like it had ever been hosted before. As I read through, I couldn't help but get excited. *Could I really do it? Become a part of sporting history?* Yes, I had shaved thirty seconds off my time in a matter of hours, but as with any athletic event, as you climb the ladder to the top, every rung gets harder to climb. The world championship standard was set at sub 5:40, meaning I'd have to run another successful beer mile faster than that to be ranked in the top ten in the world and be invited to the world championships. I left the library pondering how I could shave another fifteen seconds off my time. The bus ride home passed in a flash, and I walked in the front door to Greg sitting on the couch watching TV.

We started talking, and as the boys got home, Greg placed a six-pack of cans on the kitchen counter. He had picked them up earlier for one reason: he wanted me to perfect the chug. This is that Friday night I mentioned in Chapter Four, when we were determined to figure out the best method to chug out of a can and Greg solidified his role as my beer mile coach. Over the next two hours, I chugged a beer every twenty minutes, using a different method each time. The rules on beer-mile.com didn't state if you could squeeze the can or not, so we tried it out. Straight up vertically, straight up with a slow squeeze, straight up with a full squeeze, at a 45-degree angle, 45 degrees with a slow squeeze, and 45 degrees with a full squeeze. Greg appeared with this old-school stopwatch, like something that you would find in your grandpa's attic. There was one button on it to start, and you pushed the same button to stop. Imagine something from the first modern Olympic Games in Athens, Greece in 1896. As I write this, the same stopwatch sits in front of me on my desk; I'm surprised it hasn't run out of battery with all the use it's gotten since.

Two hours later, and a little tipsy, we had learned a lot. Through trial and error, we had found the quickest method to chugging was a slow squeeze at 45 degrees; it accelerated the flow of beer out of the can and was significantly quicker than no squeeze at all. The full squeeze made it impossible to drink the last few ounces of beer, and that wouldn't stand up to the official beer mile rules, which were getting stricter by the day. A fully vertical chug was inferior to the forty-five-degree angle; it didn't allow air to enter the can and push the beer out. Looking back, it was our first experiment with fluid dynamics.

My roommates and I then re-watched the fastest beer miles in history aside from Nielsen's 4:57. No one else who ran under 5:30 used cans; they all used bottles. *Why were they using bottles?* Eager to experiment, we grabbed a few empty beer bottles from our garage and filled them up with water, performing the same procedure as before but pouring them into the sink. It was like we were carrying out a science experiment, conducting multiple time trials of each technique in order to minimize errors in pouring or timing. The quickest we could get the 355mL/12 ounces out of a can was just under seven seconds. The quickest with bottles? Under five seconds.

This was huge! Bottles afforded an eight-second advantage across the race without any extra effort. If I could handle the speed at which the beer came out of the bottle without spilling, it would be a game changer.

The next day, I did a few chugs using beer bottles filled with water, and the difference was incredible. I couldn't wait to get on the start line again. There was only one problem: bottle size. For some reason, the standard Canadian bottle size is 341 mL, which is 14 mL or half an ounce short of the required size. Six months earlier this wouldn't have mattered, but now that race videos were uploaded to YouTube and publicly scrutinized and the beer mile was being treated as a serious event, everything had to be perfect for approval. So Greg and I searched online for hours, trying to find bottled beer available that was 355 mL and 5 percent ABV. The only bottles that were the proper size were select craft breweries and imported beers, and almost all of them didn't work for our purposes. The majority ranged from 4.5 to 4.9 percent ABV, and others were well above 6 percent and extremely hard to drink. We eventually found one that would fit all the requirements: Muskoka Cream Ale. Now, if you have never tried a cream ale, it is just like it sounds. It has a very strong taste, is extremely hoppy, and is hard to chug. However, it was the only properly sized beer we could get, so we went to the store and bought a case. I chugged two that evening and decided I would race the following week to try them out.

At this point, beer mile training could have been a full-time job, but it wasn't. I was still going to two to three classes a day, training with my team, and functioning as a regular student athlete. I made sure to have the two empty Muskoka Cream Ale bottles near the sink at all times to practice. I would wake up, eat breakfast, and do two water chugs back-to-back as quickly as I could, before running out the door to catch the bus to class. When I got back in the door in the evening after practice, I would walk straight to the sink for two more. Around 10 p.m., I would do two more, this time separately, so coach Greg, stopwatch in-hand, could time my splits. It may sound insane, but I got my bottle chug down to six seconds and change, a huge difference from about ten seconds just a week before.

Now that I had gotten my bottle chug time down, it was time for another beer mile. This would be my first one on camera, and the goal was simple: break the Ontario provincial record of 5:40 set in 1997. So that weekend, while others were sleeping in, relaxing, and preparing for the school week, I was busy trying to become one of the best beer milers in the world. *Four beers on a Sunday evening? Why not.*

I toed the line with only one competitor, my roommate, Iain. He had represented Canada multiple times in Ultimate Frisbee and enjoyed his fair share of beer, so naturally, he wanted to give the beer mile a try. We returned to the same track as before and set up. Eight Muskoka Cream Ale bottles set up on a small stool, coach Greg there to time, and another roommate, Mike, filming on his iPhone. The weather was strange: sunny with not a cloud in the sky. From inside, you would think it was a hot summer day, throw on your shorts and t-shirt, and head out the door. In reality, it was just below 30 degrees with the wind chill, so I was dressed appropriately with a hoodie, toque, and leggings on.

Mike showed the beers to the camera before we started, in order to prove to all the online critics they were beer mile legal. Greg announced, "Whenever you guys are ready . . . GO!" And we were off.

The first beer was down in about seven seconds, and I took

off at an aggressive running pace. I knew I had a great shot at the Ontario record if I could hold it together, so I was excited to get after it. I came into the second beer already breathing hard after running the last 100 meters into a direct headwind. I had the beer up for less than two seconds before having to take a break. *What was this, amateur hour?* I shook my head, knowing that if I took any more breaks, the record would certainly be out of reach. I used the frustration on lap number two, having another good run. Beer three went smooth, this time taking a few seconds before starting to chug, getting it down in one go. Lap three was a struggle, quite a bit slower than the previous two. The cream ales were not sitting well; having previously used lagers that were much lighter, I could feel the difference during this beer mile.

"Last one Lew, last one!" Greg yelled as I grabbed my last beer. This one was the easiest mentally, knowing it would all be over soon. Even though I took a quick break, I finished the last beer quickly and heard "4:30!" I knew I had to break seventy seconds over the last 400 meters to get the record, so from the first steps of the final lap, I shifted into overdrive. Sprinting the last 100 as hard as I could and leaning at the line, I heard Greg and Mike yell out a time ending in five. "5:45?" I asked with the last ounce of breath I had left. They replied, "No . . . 5:35!" I had done it.

All the training had paid off. Three weeks earlier I couldn't even have told you where the world championships were being hosted. Now I was in the running to compete there. Dozens of bottle chugs later, not only had I broken the Ontario provincial record that had stood for over seventeen years, but also run a time that could potentially get me on that start line in Austin.

I was extremely pleased with the run, and posted it online

as soon as I got home for two reasons. First, so I could get it confirmed on beermile.com and send it to FloTrack. Secondly, so I could put it up on my Facebook and give my friends something fun to watch. Within hours, the video had close to 200 likes and dozens of comments from family and friends. I couldn't believe how many people enjoyed the video; friends and acquaintances I hadn't talked to in years were messaging me saying they found it entertaining!

Once the video was posted, I drafted an email to Ryan Fenton, one of the heads of FloTrack and the person in charge of selecting the elite fields for the world championships. I included the YouTube link, explaining I had only done a handful of beer miles and knew I could go even faster if I were selected to race in Austin. I was making my case for why I deserved a spot on the start line in a matter of weeks. I went to bed with high hopes that I had done enough.

The following day, while sitting in a lecture, I pulled up the information on the FloTrack World Championships on my laptop. By the end of the two hours I couldn't tell you a single thing the professor had said; I was too busy reading up on the confirmed entries for the men's elite section.

FloTrack had released a men's race preview to build some hype before the upcoming world championships. The big headliner was Nick Symmonds, who had followed up his fifth place finish in the 800 at the London Olympics with a silver medal at the World Championships in 2013. If he could get the beers down, even at a half decent pace, he would outrun the field by a longshot.

The second major headline: no James Nielsen. After becoming the first man to break five minutes and the sole reason the beer mile went viral, he seemed to have disappeared and was not responding to any outreach. FloTrack obviously wanted him in the race, but no response meant no world record holder on the start line.

Without Nielsen in the race, this left the second fastest man of all time, Corey Gallagher, as the favorite with a personal best of 5:01. The article mentioned a few potential threats aside from Symmonds. First, the foreigner, Markus Liwing. He was flying in from Sweden for the race, and was known to be one of the best chuggers in the beer miling world. He ran his personal best of 5:24 in a field of fifty-plus runners, not only having to run around huge groups as he lapped runners, but also dressed in lederhosen head to toe. He was a character. The final athlete they mentioned was Michael Cunnigham, a New Yorker and recent UPenn grad. Cunningham was advertised as very quick, having broken four minutes in the road mile, and closing his best beer mile of 5:18 with a fifty-four-second last lap. He wasn't to be taken lightly.

Over the next few days, I couldn't get the beer mile out of my head. One afternoon, I sat down with Greg and constructed a "beer mile workout." Up until a week prior, I had only raced beer miles, practiced chugging here and there, but nothing beyond that. It was about to get a lot more intense. If I wanted to make the world championships, we were going to have to get technical. I had already run earlier that day, so the goal wasn't to get a hard effort in; instead, it was to practice chugging while out of breath and work on chugging followed by running. Since it was a Tuesday night, we decided we would try the workout using non-alcoholic beer. After a few slow laps to warm up, I did a few dynamic exercises and was ready to get going. Greg decided it would be good to do three 400 meter repeats: the first starting with a chug, the next two finishing with a chug. The entire workout took less than ten minutes, and it went great. Learning how to chug while out of breath was difficult, but I was getting better. There was one thing that would never change with the dozens of beer mile workouts I would do over the years to come: the awful taste of non-alcoholic beer. It was strange. The initial sip tasted the same as a regular beer, but the aftertaste was something else. It was uniquely awful, like watered-down rotten apple juice that had been carbonated. I wasn't a fan. However, it served its purpose for weeknights, allowing me to train without being hungover the next day.

Less than two weeks later, with all the hours of practice that I had put in, I knew I could shave off more time. Fenton had replied to my initial email informing me that I was currently in a pool of athletes being considered for the elite race. After talking with Greg, we agreed that we had put in too much work to leave it to chance; I needed to run faster and prove that I belonged on the start line in Austin. We checked, and there were four bottles left from the original case of Muskoka Cream Ale. *Perfect*. It was a Thursday night and a few guys wanted to go to the bar, so why not do a beer mile before heading out?

Conditions were similar to the previous race, just a few degrees colder as winter was rapidly approaching. I was lucky to have great roommates who were always there to support, and within a few minutes, those that were home assembled at the front door and we went over to the track. All bundled up, we had a slightly larger field this time: Phil, our friend Nick Thomas, Greg, and myself. Coach Greg figured he would be able to do his job better if he actually did a beer mile himself! Another roommate, Alex, took over timing duties for the day.

I counted us down: "Three, two, one, GO!" That was followed by the familiar noise of carbonation rushing out of the beers we were about to chug. The first two beers and laps were the same as always, smooth and quick. It was on beer three that my training really showed. I slowed down to a walk as I grabbed my beer, took a few deep breaths then got it down in one attempt. Lap three felt a bit rough, but I maintained a quick pace. After I finished beer four, Alex yelled out 4:17! I was on pace for a huge personal best and felt great. I could tell I was having a quick last lap, and with 100 meters to go, I could hear Greg yelling as loud as he could, "COME ON, LEW! LET'S GO!" He had taken a break mid race to cheer me across the line. Alex stopped the watch and announced, "5:19.9!" I had broken my own Ontario record by another sixteen seconds, and became the seventh fastest beer miler in history. It was exhilarating. *If I could run 5:19 in three layers and wearing a cape, what could I do in better conditions and with more serious competition?*

In class the next day, I felt like a zombie. Something about class at 8:30 on a Friday morning just felt wrong. Halfway through the three-hour lecture, to keep from nodding off, I decided to email Ryan Fenton to update him on my 5:19. I had rapidly gone from a guy who might not get an invite to a very serious dark horse for a medal. I was on a roll, having taken over a minute off my time in the past month, and I had no plans on slowing down. Fenton replied by the afternoon and asked if I could jump on a call. "You were running in freezing temperatures, and a cape around your neck! Can't wait to see what happens when you mix it up with the big dogs on December 3." With approval from Fenton to book my flights and accommodation in the athlete hotel covered, the issue of financing the trip was no longer a question.

Despite all that was going on, the following week started just like any other: wake up and head to class. Grab a quick lunch and head to lecture number two. From there, head to practice at 3:30. The team took off for an easy run, and after a short jog on the roads, we were into the thick of the Brescia trail. Our training log called for an easy nine miles. As usual, someone would banter away about this super cute girl they got to sit next to in a lecture or something ridiculous their roommate did the night before. The glory days of college. Everyone knew about my 5:19 from the previous week and asked me if I had booked my flight down to Austin yet. My answer to them was the truth: I wasn't sure if I was going to go. I hadn't told my parents anything about it whatsoever, and it was a pretty busy time with final papers due soon, followed by exams.

The better the conversation, the shorter the run felt, and that day the run was over before we knew it. As a team, we did a bit of stretching and then some strength work. We had started a tradition of "Spoke Tuesdays" that just meant a group of us too lazy to cook dinner would go to the campus bar to grab some food and a beer. This particular Tuesday only two of us, Chris Balestrini and me, walked from the athletic center over to the bar. Chris was in his senior year and was also a Kinesiology major. Over the past three years, we had spent countless hours together in the classroom and on the trails. On the short walk, he asked me what the chances were that I would actually fly down to Texas. I told him that I still didn't know. However, I had put in all this work, and deep down I knew I would never be able to live with all the "what if's" if I passed up on the opportunity.

We took a break from talking to eat. As usual, we inhaled our buffalo chicken wraps and fries as if we hadn't eaten in a month. We grabbed a pint and continued where our conversation left off: Was I going to fly down? FloTrack was looking to confirm the elite field by the end of the week: If I didn't book by then, my flight wouldn't be covered. Chris liked any sort of challenge, so the beer mile was no different. He opened up his laptop and said, "Let's see how much flights cost." Would he fly down with me to be a part of this once-in-a-lifetime event? I was doubtful. It was bad timing being at the end of the semester, and the event was in a matter of weeks so flights wouldn't be cheap. Regardless, he pulled up the discount flights on his laptop out of curiosity. Flights out of Detroit, only a two-hour drive away, were really affordable. I couldn't believe the next words that came out of his mouth: "I'm in." Within half an hour we had booked our flights and finalized our travel plans. Texas, here we come!

The following week was intrasquad for the varsity track team. The meet was just a series of time trials that functioned as tryouts to make the team. To add an extra element of fun and competition, the team was split into a purple team and a white team, and it was scored like a dual meet. I had competed for the team the previous year, so I was given some leeway as the coaches knew I was coming back from an injury. I was told to race if I could, and even if it went poorly, they would give me another chance in January to prove my fitness.

Cross country athletes always ran the longest indoor track event that was contested: the 3000 meter. I had only been out of the pool and running for a few weeks, so I had no expectations. Obviously, I had been doing beer miles, but that involved stopping every minute; this race was going to be nine straight minutes of agony, give or take. I typically didn't race the 3000 meter, and my personal best was still a 9:15 from high school. If you ran anything under nine minutes, you were on the team. Simple as that. I saw the race as an opportunity to tune up for the big race in Austin that was quickly approaching.

To put it in perspective, even if I had been healthy all season, I would have been lucky to be the team's seventh or eighth quickest runner. When the gun went off, I tucked in behind a group of guys I knew would be finishing right around nine minutes. My race strategy was to hold on as long as possible, then try not to get lapped by the top guys who had personal bests over thirty seconds faster than mine. I had been racing my beer miles on outdoor tracks in the brutal cold because they had to be fairly covert, and drinking wasn't permitted on our indoor track facility. The 3K race was indoors, so the early laps flew by. (Indoor tracks are 200 meters.) I didn't listen to any splits until the first kilometer when I came in at something like 2:56. I felt pretty smooth, but that was normal for early in the race. I sat at the back of the second pack, sticking to the game plan. As the next few laps went by, I couldn't believe how good I felt. We had just over a kilometer to go, and I could tell the pace of our group was slowing down, so I started to move up. By 2K I had moved to the front of the chase pack, putting me in fourth place, and heard my split of 5:56. The lead pack of three was over 75 meters in front and out of sight, so I kept grinding as they slowly came back. I remember every lap I was getting a little closer, and with 400 meters to go, they were finally within range. I was making up ground with every stride, catching up quickly, but it was just a matter of if I would run out of time. At the bell, I gave it all I had and managed to catch Phil with less than 50 meters to go and finished third. I crossed the line in disbelief. What had just happened? These guys were way out of my league even if I were in good shape!

It was definitely a combination of the guys being burnt out after a long cross country season and me somehow being fit off the beer mile time trials. Regardless, my confidence skyrocketed. Things were moving in the right direction. The time on the clock: 8:50.1, a 25-second personal best.

I decided to race the 1500 meter two days later to get in another run. This wasn't mandatory, so it was only a field of four, but I took the lead early and was able to go gun to tape, winning by a few seconds. My confidence was growing every time I stepped on the track.

I went home that evening on such a high note, still in shock of what had just happened. It was then that I decided it was finally time. I had contemplated talking to my parents before booking my flight; then, on impulse, booked with Chris. It had been a number of days since I booked, and I still couldn't think of a way to tell them. Neither of them knew the first thing about the beer mile. My mom would be intrigued and supportive, as long as I was safe, which I would be. However, I knew my dad would be harder to crack. He worked for the municipal government, so he couldn't condone the drinking on public property that was necessary for the beer mile. I decided there was no better way to open the conversation than with how well my race had just gone. I clicked the FaceTime icon, and my dad immediately picked up. Cue the conversation that started this chapter, with my dad walking away to process while I talked to my mom.

"Texas?! Beer mile?" My mom was more open to the idea than my dad. She was intrigued and excited and saw a cool opportunity for me. I can talk for hours on end about pretty much anything, and I get that from my mom. She asked me to back up the story and give her the full rundown. Half an hour later, she was fully informed.

"Between you and me, that sounds awesome. I'll work on your father, he'll get over it. He just needs some time to process it." She did what mothers do best, comfort and resolve the situation.

After I got off FaceTime with my parents, I felt a lot more

confident that I had the support of my mom and knew my dad would come around. I reviewed the travel plans and realized we would only be in Austin for forty hours, leaving the minute I finished my final lecture of the semester and arriving back the evening before the first exam. Travelling across the continent to drink beer and run—it was unbelievable. Even if I finished dead last, it was going to be an unforgettable trip.

# CHAPTER SIX

# Everything's Bigger in Texas

OUR FLIGHTS WERE out of Detroit, which was right across the Canadian border from Windsor, a two-hour drive. Luckily, one of my childhood best friends, Joe Kagumba, had offered us a place to stay the night before, plus a ride across the border to the airport the following day. Throughout high school, Joe and I had spent hundreds of hours together running, at parties, and just hanging out. He lived with a few teammates, and as expected when we arrived at his place around 9 p.m., we found it was a classic college runner's house. The walls of the common room didn't have a single inch that wasn't covered in running or beer posters. Some of the group were huddled around a TV playing *Super Smash Bros.*, while the others sat back cracking jokes. They knew all about the world championships and couldn't believe in less than forty-eight hours I would be racing Nick Symmonds. Looking back, I still hadn't realized how cool it was going to be. Everything was happening so fast. Around midnight we called it a night, and I was glad to hear there was a spare bed; I wasn't expecting anything more than a couch or a floor to crash on.

The next morning, Joe drove Chris and me across the border to the airport in Detroit. Our flight departed at 1:50 p.m., with a layover in Charlotte, North Carolina, to get to Austin at 6:15 p.m. The travel day was smooth; it passed by quickly between sleeping and thinking about the race the next day. Ryan Fenton told me to call him when I landed to arrange a shuttle to the hotel. Our suitcases were the first to come off the carousel, just as the shuttle pulled up. After a short drive, we arrived at the Holiday Inn where we were staying.

We walked in the front door and lined up to check in. I had been told a few days before that I would be rooming with Markus Liwing, the Swedish guy who raced in lederhosen. FloTrack had announced he had set the beer half marathon world record the day before. Thirteen beers and thirteen miles in two hours and forty-six minutes! He was definitely a little wild, so I was certain we would get along well. It was getting late, and we still had to get a shakeout run in and eat dinner. Once we got our room keys, we walked around the corner and jumped in the elevator. I had built up this image of Markus in my head after seeing his beer mile and reading a few of his interviews. Would he live up to expectations? I knocked on the door, to the warm welcome of not only Markus but three of his Swedish friends. I had already told Chris he could stay in our room; would there now be six of us between two queen beds? That would just add to the story. Luckily, Markus's friends had booked the room next door, so it wasn't an issue.

Chris and I dropped our stuff, got into our running gear, and left the hotel for an easy three-mile jog. By this time it was pitch black, and the smart decision would have been to run on the well-lit sidewalks. It's safe to say that sometimes we weren't the best at making the smart decisions. The Swedes told us there was a soft dirt path that you could run on for miles that ran on both sides of a nearby lake, and it was less than 100 meters from the front door of our hotel. We couldn't resist the temptation and took off for the dirt path. Regardless of the fact that we were barely able to see our feet below us, the pace was crisp. I love running at night. When it's dark out and there aren't distractions all around, I find I get into the zone and feel light on my feet. We finished up our three miles with some strides out in front of the hotel. I was so hungry I could eat a horse.

The Swedes had waited for us, so after a quick shower, we walked to the closest restaurant for a late dinner. It was on Rainey Street, a historic district made up of approximately two dozen bungalow-style homes that had been repurposed as bars and an entertainment district. It was the definition of hipster. We sat down at the first place we saw and immediately ordered food and a round of beers. The dimly lit room echoed with conversation, and we all shared our stories of how we ended up in Texas. Markus and his friends had wanted to come to the US for a while, and this beer mile was the perfect excuse for a vacation to the US. They had been to a few cities before the race and would continue on to a few others afterward, all part of a three-week-long trip.

It was getting late, so we finished our food and drinks and started walking back to the hotel. As we did, Markus asked if we had seen his race preparation video from earlier that day. *What had he done now?* With a GoPro strapped to his head, Markus did a mini beer mile in the hallway of our hotel. We were in a tower that only had ten rooms on each floor in a circular fashion, with the elevator in the middle. Markus figured each lap was only about thirty meters, so he proceeded to chug three beers, with three laps of the hall between each. We laughed the entire video long, which went to his head camera on four-times speed when he was running, then would cut to his friend filming on a phone when he chugged. He then challenged to see if us Canadians could beat the Swedes' times. Once again, I couldn't say no to the challenge. Chris and I grabbed a few Coronas from the gas station across the street and copied Markus's race exactly. GoPro on head and all. We were fully-grown men, running around hotel hallways like we were in grade school again. As I grabbed my last beer, the hotel receptionist came out of the elevator and asked what we were doing. I told her we would only be one more minute, chugged my beer and took off for my last few laps. She had come upstairs due to a noise complaint but was so confused about what she just witnessed that she wasn't even mad. In the end, we didn't even compare times. Running around the halls in skin tight singlets and shorts shorter than most people would consider appropriate, it was completely ridiculous. Finally, it was time for bed, with one final sleep before the big day.

I woke up in the middle of the night to go to the bathroom; must have been all the bottle chugs before bed. It was 3 a.m., and as I got back into bed, my phone light came on with a notification; an email from Ryan Fenton: "BEER MILE UPDATE: Venue Change & Rules." I read part of the email but was still half asleep, I so decided just to go back bed and figure it out in the morning.

A few hours later, my alarm went off and I had completely forgotten about the email, having cleared the notification in the middle of the night. Chris, Markus, and I went down to the continental breakfast in the hotel lobby. It was only once we sat down at the table with a few of the other elite athletes that I remembered the email. I pulled it back up to get more details. Issues had arisen with the original venue, a local high school track, so FloTrack had to make last minute arrangements. The race would now be hosted at the Circuit of the Americas, regarded by many as the best Formula One racing track in the world. In other words, the profile of the event just went through the roof. The email concluded with a clear statement: "While this may change some of variables, this does not change what this event is—a race for a World Championship." Something about that last sentence resonated with me. I was 1,600 miles from home, and I couldn't wait to be on that start line surrounded by a roaring crowd, jumbotrons, and the best beer milers in the world. There was only one issue: most of us racing had only brought track spikes. The metal pins in the bottom of these shoes would not work on the new concrete race surface.

Once I finished up breakfast, I had one task before the athlete meeting at noon: pick up the beers I wanted to race with. I didn't fly down with any Muskoka Cream Ale, so I was going to have to find a new beer. Corey Gallagher had announced he would use Bud Light Platinum, as he found it the easiest to get down. Despite being 6 percent ABV, they were really low carbonation and didn't take as much of a toll on the stomach, which was essential in the beer mile. Chris and I made a quick trip to the local store where there were plenty of beer options, but Bud Light Platinum seemed like the right one. We were instructed to bring a twelve-pack of our beer of choice to the technical meeting.

By the time we got back to the hotel, it was time to head to the conference room to go over the details of the race. I had never been part of anything like it before. The room was filled with the best beer milers in the world, coming from all sorts of backgrounds. A couple of the world's fastest runners, a few of the world's fastest chuggers, and a lot of people in between. I definitely fell into the third category.

As soon as everyone took their seats, Fenton handed us all our individual race kits. Inside was our race number and the set of rules. Before beginning the meeting, we were told that Hops and Grain, the event's beer sponsor, had brewed a "beer mile" beer specifically for the race. It was beer mile legal but had about a third of the carbonation of a regular beer. It would be a massive risk to race with as no one had ever tried it before. The other major issue: it was only available in a can. They had a case available at the meeting and most athletes grabbed one to test it out. By the end of the meeting, we had to decide if we wanted to use the twelve-pack we brought or the Hops and Grain provided. The tension in the room rose as everyone knew this could make or break their shot at a world title. The meeting moved on, and Fenton introduced Patrick Butler from beermile.com, whom they had flown in to clarify the official set of rules (opposite).

At the meeting, a major topic of discussion was if squeezing the can was allowed. Butler decided it was illegal, as it accelerated the flow of beer and that went against rule seven: "Beer cans must not be tampered with in any manner." The funniest question needing clarification was one regarding at what point you were allowed to throw up. Someone asked, "If it happens after I have officially crossed the line, I know I'm good. But what if I'm in my final steps and it lands beyond the finish line, am I good?" The room broke out in laughter. It was a ridiculous question but had to be clarified now in case that scenario actually did occur. The consensus was that

# OFFICIAL FLO RULES

## Modified Kingston / Beermile.com Rules

Note: see rule 11 for noteworthy "flo" rules modification

1 – Competitors must be at least 21 years of age on day of competition.

2 – Each competitor drinks four cans (or bottles) of beer and runs four laps on a track. Start - beer/lap, beer/lap, beer/lap, beer/lap - Finish

3 – Beer must be consumed before the lap has begun, within the transition area. (The 10-meter zone before the start/finish line)

4 – The race begins with the drinking of the first beer in the last meter of the transition zone. This ensures the competitors run a complete mile.

5 – Competitors must drink cans or bottles of beer and the contents will be no less than 12 ounces. Bottles may be substituted for cans as long as they are at least 12 ounces (355 mL) in volume.

6 – No specialized cans or bottles may be used that give an advantage by allowing the beer to pour at a faster rate. "Super mega mouth cans" or "vortex bottles" and other such containers are prohibited.

7 – Beer cans must not be tampered with in any manner. No shotgunning or puncturing of the can except for opening the can by the tab at the top. The same applies with bottles—no straws or other aids are allowed in order to aid in the speed of pouring.

8 – Beer must be a minimum of 5 percent alcohol by volume.

9 – The beer must be a fermented alcoholic beverage brewed from malt and flavored with hops.

10 – Each beer can or bottle must not be opened until the competitor enters the transition zone on each lap.

*11 – Competitors who vomit before they finish the race will be DISQUALIFIED.

your chest had to cross the line and the clock stop before you could throw up at all. The final thing I remember from the meeting was that Corey Gallagher tried to get Butler to strip James Nielsen of the world record. He brought up a few good arguments, the strongest being that Nielsen drank his second beer in just under four seconds, which is literally impossible unless you tamper with the can. "If you can show me a video of anyone in the world drinking a can in four seconds—it doesn't even have to be James Nielsen—I'll shut up." Even with Gallagher's solid argument and consensus in the room that the 4:57 was sketchy, Butler couldn't go back on his decision to ratify the world record from earlier that year.

Mid-meeting, I texted Greg, who was back in Ontario, and we decided even if the customized beer was good, the cans would be too much of a change after all the bottle chugs, so I stuck with what worked. I handed in my twelve-pack of Bud Light Platinums on the way out of the athlete meeting. Aware that the last minute venue change caused a footwear problem, FloTrack shuttled a group of us that had only brought spikes to the local running store to pick up some racing flats. Luckily, they had the exact same pair of flats I trained in back home. At least they would be a familiar fit. We got back to the hotel with a few hours to spare before heading to the race course.

I lay down in my bed to relax and thought for a moment how crazy all this was. New shoes, new beer, and a new venue. So many things could go wrong, or it could all go according to plan. Despite the intensity of the day, I somehow fell asleep knowing the gun would be off in a matter of hours and tens of thousands of people would tune in live to see the crowning of the first ever beer mile world champion.

Chris woke me up at 4:30 p.m., knowing we had to be in the lobby for the 5 p.m. shuttle over to the Circuit of the

Americas. Everyone was making small talk as we boarded the mini-bus over to the course. Everyone was very laid back—not what you would expect from athletes about to compete for a world title. I didn't know most of the people we were in the shuttle with, so I listened as they explained their stories. Everyone was either Canadian or American, with the addition of Markus and the Swedes. While some specialized in the mile and others were marathoners, the beer mile had brought together people from across the world. This would become a recurring theme in the international beer miles to follow.

The twenty-minute drive passed quickly, and we arrived at the race course to a massive banner about fifty feet long that read "FloTrack Beer Mile World Championships." The course was a 400-meter loop on the actual F1 race track. The straightaways were about 150 meters long, making for sharp 50-meter turns. Chris and I went to the registration area where we picked up our race packages. There were three sections of open races that anyone could run in before the championship races, so Chris entered in the middle section. My package included an elite athlete pass, so Chris and I used that to get into the VIP area that was set up for the elites to be able to sit down and relax. The press floated around, and I overheard the headliner athletes do a bunch of interviews. I was pinning my race number to my singlet when someone sitting nearby spoke up. I was excited to recognize Jim Finlayson from all the research I had done on who I would be racing. "You're too young to have that singlet!" he joked. I had gotten the vintage Athletics Canada singlet off my university coach, Guy Schultz, and explained that to Jim. It turns out they knew each other well and had quite the rivalry back in the late nineties. It really is a small world. After a bit more small talk, we went out to spectate a few races before it was time to warm up.

Before the women's elite race started, the Men's Sub-Elite competed. This race featured the men who could run under 6:15 but not quite at the sub 5:40 cut off for the Elite section. The matchup from the gun was Jeff Mountjoy, a Canadian, and Lon Brittenbach, an American. Jeff Mountjoy was easily identifiable: his long beard and Canada shirt identified one of the most entertaining individuals I have ever met. Jeff won the first beer mile I had ever run in 5:52. At that race, I had crossed the line in 6:11 and couldn't understand how I came fifth in what I thought was an incredible debut time. Now a few months later, Jeff and I were no longer competing in front of a few dozen of our friends, but in front of a live audience of a thousand or so, and countless tuning in online. Lon Brittenbach had announced he would be going after the Super Masters—age forty and over—world record.

The entire field used Hops and Grain cans, as only the elite fields were allowed to use bottles. Brittenbach was off the line first with an 8.2-second chug, and about a dozen others were done under twelve seconds. The announcers told the crowd Lon had been training to get his speed up to break the record. Brittenbach went into the second beer with a five-second lead and made quick work of beer two. Mountjoy was ten seconds back going into lap two but looked smooth. By the third beer, Mountjoy had the gap down to just three seconds. Brittenbach got his beer down very quickly, with a questionable amount of spillage and received a warning from the head judge. Mountjoy once again closed the gap on lap three and for the first time in the race took the lead grabbing his fourth beer. Brittenbach outdrank Mountjoy by a few seconds, once again spilling quite a bit. Mountjoy stayed composed and didn't spill a drop. Slowly closing the gap, he blew by Brittenbach over the last 100 meters, cruising to victory in 5:38. Brittenbach came in at 5:42, a Super Master's world record by nine seconds! After the race, Mountjoy had a live interview, broadcasted over the jumbotron for the audience in the stadium and tuned in online. To date, it is the greatest post-race interview I have ever heard. When asked, "What is your favorite training technique?" he responded, "Well . . . sometimes I drink a pitcher as fast as I can. My quickest without puking is just under a minute." Mountjoy was an amazing ambassador for the emerging, extremely entertaining sport.

After watching the men's sub-elite race from the sidelines, I gave my Canadian flag to Chris and took off to warm up with Jim Finlayson. I had brought down the flag hoping to cross that line in a podium position and hold it up as I had seen so many Olympians do over the years. Up and down the Formula One track, it is still to this day one of the coolest warm ups I have ever done. Jim and I watched the women's race on the jumbotron as we chatted away and warmed up.

Unlike the diverse men's field, the women's field was almost entirely made up of Americans. The group of women, all using cans, were dead even after the first beer. On the back straight, Elizabeth Laseter charged to the front, clearly wanting to set a fast pace. She came into the second beer a couple of seconds ahead of the pack. All of the women swarmed into the chug zone, battling to grab their beers. Andrea Fisher, a local and distinguished triathlete, had the quickest chug and led going into lap two. The field strung out, and only half the women remained in contention. Chris Kimborough, pre-race favorite and mother of six, took the lead going into beer three. Fisher once again had the best chug and led going into lap three, but Kimborough and Beth Herdonen were close behind. Fisher held the lead for half the lap before Herdonen breezed by. Through the final chug and lap, she never looked back. Crossing the line in a new world record of 6:17, she shattered the old record of 6:28. Early on, she stayed composed, and one by one the rest of the field seemed to fall apart around her. Arms over her head, she smiled across the line, and why wouldn't she? She just won $5,000 to run four laps and chug four beers! I remember getting to the start line to a flurry of cameras around her, and she was a ball of joy. *Damn*, I thought, *what I would do to be in her shoes.*

We had been told to be in the elite athlete recruiting area twenty minutes prior to race start, so I headed over there to switch into my flats. I took off my warm-up track pants with a sense of pride. Coach Guy had also given me a pair of his Team Canada track pants. Outdated and retro, the shiny red pants had golden maple leafs down the side and stood out. Rightfully so, they were from the early 1990s. As usual, when I went to sit down to change shoes, I began to sweat profusely. I don't know if this happens to every runner, but I knew it was a good sign. The body was warmed up and ready to go, but it was time to strip down to the racing kit. Growing up, I had always dreamed of one day representing Canada. This wasn't at all how I imagined it would be—it was way better. In the days leading up, I had dozens of family and friends reach out to wish me good luck. I felt like I wasn't only racing for myself, but for a nation filled with beer-loving runners.

I went to the massive fridge cooler where the race organizers were storing our beers and took mine out. Nice and cold, just how I liked them. I placed them on my pre-determined spot on the chug tables and did some warm-up drills. In less than fifteen minutes, I would be on that start line, and a few minutes later, a world champion would be crowned. Would it be me? Likely not. Gallagher had been training for this moment for months. As the fastest man on the start line, with a personal best of 5:01, and also one of the most experienced beer milers in the world, he was the heavy favorite. Then I remember thinking, *Who knows what will happen?* The risk of having a bad day in the beer mile is double that of a regular race. Typically, if your legs, lungs, and mental game are on point, you are set up for success. However, even if those are all primed, in the beer mile, you can have a major problem: your stomach.

I stopped thinking about everyone else on the line and focused on myself for a moment. There I was, standing on the world famous Circuit of the Americas, the Grand-Prix track where Sebastian Vettel and Lewis Hamilton had stood, alongside world-class car companies like Ferrari and Mercedes. Where global stars like Jimmy Buffet and Paramore had performed, and where Kanye West and Drake would play in the years to come. *How did I manage to get here?*

My thought was interrupted as two guys dressed in banana suits ran by, dancing around. It was all so ridiculous. If you told me a month ago that I would be on this start line, I would have asked you what planet you were on.

I was standing there, ready to take on the world. In a handful of beer miles, I had brought my time down from 6:22 to 5:19. If anyone on the start line had a chance to be a true dark horse or underdog for a podium finish, it was me. This is actually a tactic I employ before every race, a way to get myself fired up and excited to go for it. I never saw it as pressure, all my family and friends as well as thousands of strangers watching me live. It was an opportunity to shock the world, to make my mark in beer mile history. In the words of a man I hadn't met yet, Kris Mychasiw, "If she dies, she dies."

It felt like I was a professional athlete. The top ten men in the world were on the start line, and I was one of them. There was no reason I couldn't come away with a medal. Yes, I was one of the least experienced in the field, but that was motivation for me: I had been cutting off big chunks of time every time I raced, so what was stopping me from doing it again? As multiple massive cameras panned across the start line, the race announcers named the athletes one by one. I will never forget when they called my name. I waved to the camera, knowing I had at least fifty friends and family across the world tuned in to watch. Of course, I was a little nervous, but more than anything, I was excited. I couldn't believe the fury of events that had occurred in the past six weeks.

Before I knew it, the starter called us to the line, "On your marks!" The horn sounded, and it was just like all those times Greg said GO! The first beer was gone before I could blink, and I was in third place off the line. However, the entire field was within a few seconds of each other and instantly packed up. While Gallagher had the lead off the line, Tully Hannan, an American, flew by on the back straight to take a big lead going into beer number two. I felt good on lap one but wasn't used to being surrounded by so many other runners. Grabbing my second beer was a struggle; it felt like a full-contact sport. The second beer went down great, and I was sitting in fourth place heading into lap number two. I fell into sixth place on the second lap as the naturally faster runners passed me, including Olympian Nick Symmonds. However, I was still only a few seconds back of third place and felt confident that I could out-drink the rest of the field. My third beer was where I started to hit some trouble. I once again struggled to navigate the field to grab my beer, and even once I managed to grab it, it was the furthest thing from smooth. Having to take a breath at half way, I fell into seventh place before taking off for lap three. Up ahead of me, it had become a two-horse race: Cunningham leading the way with quicker laps with Gallagher close behind and gaining lots of ground on the chugs. Lap three I definitely started to feel weighed down by the beer but managed to pass Symmonds and Anderson. They must have been hurting more than me. When I got to beer four, I found it to be worse than beer three; I was really struggling and needed to take a four- or five-second break to burp and catch my breath. I was sitting in fourth going into the final lap. Later on, I would find out that Jack Colreavy had puked on beer four, disqualifying him from the race. I was in a lot of discomfort on lap four; all I can remember is every few steps I would try to burp to release some of the built-up carbonation and all I was getting up was foam. The damn Bud Light Platinums got me! I was determined to make it across the line without puking, so I had to slow my pace in order to not get disqualified. I ran the final 100 meters with my neck cranked up to the sky because I knew I was going to throw up—I just had to get across the line first. After the final lap that felt longer than a marathon, I crossed the line, and all four beers came back up in a foamy gross texture.

When I was done puking, Chris ran over to me, "Lew, you were fifth!" At first, I saw my time of 5:32 and was extremely disappointed. Jim Finlayson had finished third in 5:21. If I had just run the same time I had a few weeks prior, I would have been on the podium. Corey Gallagher had broken away from Cunningham over the last lap to win easily and be crowned the inaugural world champion in 5:00. I'm not a negative person at all, but I was in a sour mood until I got back to my bag and checked my phone. I opened it to dozens of texts and Facebook messages from friends and family: "You just beat the world silver medalist in the 800m! Way to go man." Or "Lew, that was the most entertaining thing I have ever watched. You're fifth in the world!" It only took a few messages and a few minutes to turn my mood around. No, I didn't get a medal, nor did I have the perfect race. But I was 1,600 miles from home and had just taken part in the most fun race of my life. Eight weeks before, I was a nobody in the beer mile world, and now I had beaten some of the best of all time, not to mention one of the best middle distance runners in US history.

Tully and I grouped together for a quick ten-minute cool down just so the legs would feel a bit better the next day, then Chris and I found Markus and the Swedes, and we jumped on the shuttle back to the hotel. We showered quick and cabbed to the afterparty that FloTrack had organized. Elite athletes got free beer! The night was incredible, getting to know everyone a little better. I even got to spend some time chatting with Symmonds. How many people can say they have sat down with a world silver medalist and Olympian for a beer and talked for an hour? I brought along an old singlet, and I had the entire men's elite field sign it. Today it hangs in the corner of my room, and while most people couldn't interpret the drunken chicken scratch, I could tell you all about the man behind every signature. We partied into the early morning, as was expected.

When we sat down at breakfast the next morning, the mood was incredible despite how hungover we all were. We had just been part of history. Someone asked the table where we thought the event could go from here. Jim Finlayson, the legend himself, said that he believed this was the peak. It wasn't negative, just realistic: that the underground event had been shown on the global stage, we all had our time to shine, and it would go back to its origin of college students sneaking onto moonlit tracks, racing for glory within their friend group, not for $5,000 on a live stream, with tens of thousands of people tuned in. A few others had differing opinions. I saw two possible outcomes. Either this event would never happen again, or this time next year I was going to have to be a hell of a lot faster if I even wanted to get invited, let alone stand on the podium. (Luckily for me, the latter became a reality.) Chris and I took the hotel shuttle back to the airport, and before we knew it, we were boarding our flight back to Canada.

I looked out the window as we took off and reflected on the last five weeks. None of it would have been possible without the support of so many key people: my parents for agreeing not to disown me and my roommates for challenging me to something I couldn't say no to; Chris for giving me the final nudge and joining me on a trip of a lifetime; and dozens of family and friends for reaching out with words of support and encouragement. I hoped this would be the first adventure of many.

# CHAPTER SEVEN

# Anything for a Free T-Shirt

I TIED MY shoes in a double knot and closed the door behind me. As always, the first few miles after time off felt anything but smooth. The crisp spring weather was a sign that the long, harsh winter was behind us. Soon enough my teammates and I would be running around the city in nothing but split shorts. Usually, in March, I would sit down with my coach and set specific goals for a summer full of racing on the track and the roads, but not this year. My knee injury had held me to only three to four days of running a week indoors, and the only goal I had for the summer was to slowly build back up to running six days a week again. I wanted everything to be feeling good going into my senior year cross country season.

Taking advantage of the nice weather, I ran into the nearby Brescia forest, which hadn't been an option all winter because of snow. We were lucky to have a forest full of dirt trails at our fingertips. The muddy terrain was not conducive for speed, which gave me a great excuse to run at a pedestrian pace. As I slipped and struggled up a long hill, I reflected on the indoor season that had just passed. It was my best indoor season to date, setting personal bests in every distance I contested. I seemed to have a new bounce in my step for both training and racing. The atmosphere of a short trip to Austin had completely changed the way I looked at running. Don't get me wrong, I was a dedicated collegiate athlete prior to the beer mile. However, my newly-found talent gave me extra motivation to get to that next level. If I could run quicker, I wouldn't just be competing for a spot on my collegiate championship team, I would be inching closer to being able to go head to head with the best beer milers in the world. On the days I didn't want to run, I visualized being back on that start line at the world championships. Standing under the big lights, surrounded by dozens of cameras with thousands of people watching live. The roar of the crowd as they called us to the start line. The adrenaline rushing through my body as I thought maybe, just maybe, I could pull off the upset and win the whole damn thing. There was no day too busy, no winter storm too cold that could keep me from getting out the door.

There was something about the first few weeks back to training that I thoroughly enjoyed. While I always liked to have a race to look towards, not having one in the immediate future felt relaxing. For the first two weeks back to running in March, there were no prescribed workouts; it was all easy, slow mileage to get the body adjusted back to the training load. Workouts were slowly and carefully phased into the following weeks, but we wouldn't step foot on the track until the end of April. Before that happened, we would have to endure weeks

RUN RESPONSIBLY.

A photo shoot taken by the *Western News* after the beer mile exploded into local and international media. My student newspaper took my fun trip and made a serious point.
*Credit: Frank Neufeld,* Western News

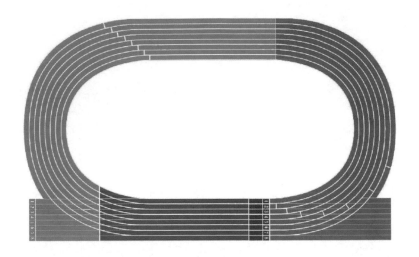

Instructional diagram for Chapter 3:
  Orange = Medium effort for first 100m
  Green = GO, harder effort for middle 200m
  Red = Slow down, take it easy for next 91m into the chug zone
  Black = 9m of chug zone
*Credit: Hunter Andrin*

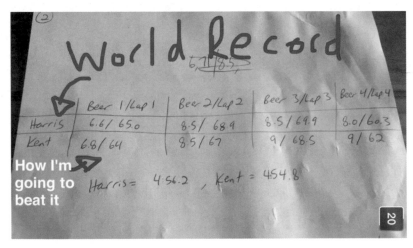

Snapchat screenshot reference from Chapter 4 of Josh Harris's world record video, tracked his split times, and planned how I was going to break it. *Credit: Photo courtesy of the author*

The race directors presenting me with the "Champion's Shoe" for winning the 2015 Toronto Spring Beer Mile while wearing the shirt that attracted me to the race in the first place.
*Credit: Jess Baumung*

Seconds after the gun went off at the 2015 Beer Mile World Classic. *Credit: Taylor Gilkeson*

Leading the pack at the 2015 Beer Mile World Classic. *Credit: Taylor Gilkeson*

The pint glass that sat in front of Kris Mychasiw when he first called me. He couldn't imagine a better partnership than with a brand like Brooks: "Run Happy to Live Lager!" *Credit: Kris Mychasiw*

The start line of the 2015 FloTrack Beer Mile World Championships. *Photo Credit: Caleb Kerr*

From the start of the race, I had my eyes on the prize (and my beer). *Credit: Caleb Kerr*

Celebrating the world title in proper fashion, drinking a beer from the Champion's trophy. *Credit: Caleb Kerr*

Moments after winning the 2015 FloTrack Beer Mile World Championships, I was pulled aside for an interview and handed the trophy while enjoying my cool-down beer. *Credits: Caleb Kerr*

This shot was for a photo shoot for *The Walrus*, featuring Ph... me, and a surprise furry friend.
*Credit: Rhiannon Russell*

A photo from a 2017 issue of *Runner's World* where they featured me and the beer mile.
*Credit: Francisco Garcia*

Another photo from the 2017 *Runner's World* feature.
*Credit: Francisco Garcia*

The podium of the 2017 Brooks International Beer Mile. From left to right: Melissa Vandewater (race director), Michael Whitehead (third place finisher), me, and Josh Harris (runner-up). *Credit: Melissa Vandewater*

An up close view of the custom made Brooks Beer Mile Hyperion. Branded red and white to reflect my Canadian heritage and gold for my world champion title. *Credit: Francisco Garcia*

of longer intervals and tempo runs to build up an aerobic base, which is crucial for success on the track.

However, there was one reason every April my teammates and I stepped on the track before the training schedule called for it: The annual Schlitz Genuine Gold Beer Mile Classic in Hamilton, Ontario. Why the name? Nobody knows.

The event was a great way to bring together a group that usually only competed sans beer for a less serious race followed by a big party to celebrate the end of yet another season. The year before, 2014, I had barely known what the beer mile was—a lot had changed since then. I went into that race unsure if I would be able finish, now fast forward 365 days, and I was not only the favorite, but everyone expected me to blow the competition out of the water. My teammates and I left London only a couple of hours before the race was set to start, as Hamilton was only a short drive away. Once we arrived, we parked, dropped our stuff off at a friend's house where we would crash later that evening, and got into our race kits. For me, that meant a toque, gloves, a long-sleeved shirt and hoodie on top, and, despite the freezing temperatures, split shorts. Plus, my signature green cape to top it all off. We tied up our shoes and ran out the door to meet the group assembling at the track.

We got to the track assuming we were the first ones there until we heard voices across the field. It was dark enough that I could barely see ten feet in front of me, but we followed the noise until we came to a group of forty or so. The mood was upbeat: it was exciting and terrifying all at the same time. In a matter of seconds, we would be chugging beers and flying around the track. This was a far cry from the official beer mile a few months ago in Austin which had tables, officials, a massive audience, and prize money on the line. The track was covered in over one hundred beers, and with no way to officiate, the honor system was in place. There was a handful of spectators present, and the prize was greater than money: bragging rights until next year.

One of the spectators counted us down. "TEN, NINE, EIGHT . . ." everyone standing on the start line went silent. "THREE, TWO, ONE, GO!" The silence was broken by the noise of carbonation rushing out of freshly opened beers. As usual, I finished my first beer before I could even think about it. By this point I had done hundreds of practice chugs; the act was automatic. My race strategy was simple: make the pace hard early. At first it made no sense. The other guys in contention were fitter, why try to outrun them? Well, they were all decent beer drinkers too, so if the pace was slow, I wouldn't gain much ground on them in the chug zone. If I was within their striking distance on the last lap, one of them would surely sprint me down and take the win.

In distance races, quite often it isn't the fittest athlete on the line who wins, but the one who tactically runs the best race. Whether that fact applies to the beer mile or not is still in question, but for this race, it held true.

I ran the first 200 meters at a ridiculously fast pace to build an early lead. Between the pitter-patter of steps on the track and the sound of loud, uncontrollable burps, I knew there was a group close behind me. Early feelings of oxygen debt were setting in after only 400 meters, but I was confident I could stay composed. While the beers still weren't a walk in the park for me, the rest of the field struggled, taking breaks to burp and breathe. From there on out, every lap I could feel the group behind me thin out until I chugged my fourth beer and took off running for the final time. I rounded the last corner onto the back straight and for a moment there was nothing but silence. That is, until I passed two runners still on their third lap who had pulled onto the infield to throw up together. *Who said the beer mile wasn't about camaraderie?* I brought it home the last hundred meters, finishing in a time of 5:31. The group of guys that beat me last year followed shortly behind, with a handful finishing under six minutes. The cut-off for the elite section at World Championships was 5:48; I found it incredible that four or five guys that all lived in southwestern Ontario ran that fast on a pitch black track in bone-chilling conditions. It seemed Canadians had a real knack for this beer mile thing.

The remainder of the field rolled in, with the poor soul who finished last clocking in around twenty-four minutes. By the time we'd thrown all the beer cans and bottles into garbage bins, everyone was eager to get back to some warmth and excited for a long night of good times ahead. As we jogged back to the party, I realized that in less than forty-eight hours, high school students would be having their track and field practice where dozens of people just painted the track with their dinner. For their sakes, I really hope it rained the next day.

On the drive back to London, we talked about how many people both inside and outside the running community were attracted to the entertainment the beer mile offered. While not everyone wanted to run it themselves, a lot of people found the beer mile more interesting to watch than a regular mile. Someone jokingly threw out the idea that it would be fun to watch a beer mile training series Rocky Balboa style—minus the meat punching bags, and adding in a few adult beverages.

The idea sounded like it could work: get the insider view of Lewis Kent as he edges closer to breaking five minutes in the beer mile. There was only one issue. How would I actually train for it? Yes, people had been running beer miles for over twenty years now, but no one had ever broken it down to a science. We all liked to joke that enjoying a few too many beers on a Saturday night was beer mile training but if that actually prepared you for the race remained to be seen. Up to this point, to get better at the beer mile, people simply ran more beer miles. We changed that forever by putting our heads together and breaking down how to improve our chances of success in each part of the race.

The following weeks were filled with excitement. My friends and I pitched a three-part documentary series, "The Road to Sub 5," to the owner of Trackie.ca, Adam Stacey. Trackie was the biggest running website in Canada. It posted content, hosted forums, and big running fans checked it daily. He loved the idea. Time to get filming.

We were going to need a whole film crew to pull this off, but seeing as we didn't have an action-movie-sized budget, our roommates would have to do. Later, the seven of us sat down at our kitchen table and brainstormed the blueprint for the series. I was lucky to live with a group of guys who were all creative and ridiculous but not afraid to speak up when they thought an idea flat out wouldn't work. After weeks of filming, hundreds of takes, and dozens of hours of video editing— thanks, Phil—we had a final product. Adam Stacey decided it would be best to post one episode per week to build anticipation, in hopes to build up a dedicated beer mile audience.

We started by releasing a teaser video that previewed the series to follow. It began with a first-person view of me waking up to four non-alcoholic beers on my bedside dresser, then chugging them all back to back. No one would actually believe this was my morning routine, would they? It was utterly absurd, but that was the basis of the entire series. The

rest of the video featured short clips of us running and concluded with an aerial drone shot. People love drone footage.

The first episode featured everything that encompassed
beer mile training. A vast majority of it consisted of practicing
the chug. Depending on the day, my liquid of choice could be
water, non-alcoholic beer, or, if I was lucky, a real beer. One
thing was certain: a day didn't go by that I wasn't completing
at least six chugs.

Beyond that, Greg and I did some research on how professional eaters prepare for their competitions. If you've never
seen footage of a hot dog eating contest, please stop reading
for a moment and Google it. As of this writing, Joey Chestnut
holds the world record, eating seventy-four hotdogs and buns
in ten minutes! Now that is absolutely ridiculous, but there is
a point of comparison. If Joey Chestnut trained his stomach
to be able to hold that many hotdogs, four beers should be a
breeze. While I didn't even come close to the extremes he did,
one of his techniques in particular sparked my interest: eating
an entire watermelon. Watermelon is not only a tasty snack,
but it's also 92 percent water, making it perfect for training as
when it is being digested in your stomach, it expands. Greg
and Iain decided to join in, so the three of us sat down at
the kitchen table with three massive watermelons. Averaging
about twelve pounds in weight each, ninety minutes later, and
after many moments of doubt and regret had passed, we did
it. However, the biggest surprise came when I woke up seven
times in the middle of the night to go to the bathroom. I
may as well have drunk four liters of water right before bed.
It made for a miserable sleeping experience, but it would all
prove to be worth it a few days later.

Episode two is easily the most ridiculous thing I have ever
attempted. Before heading down to Texas the previous fall, I

was watching video after video of the fastest beer miles ever run when I stumbled upon something a bit different: Josh Harris's "beer two-mile." It was exactly as it sounds. Eight laps broken up by eight beers. If one beer mile wasn't enough of a challenge, why not do them back to back? With the total volume consumed almost three liters, a ninth (penalty for vomiting) lap was inevitable. Harris broke the world record in a time of 14:27. I knew if I tried the beer two-mile that it would turn heads. There was no way I could properly prepare for it; I just had to get out there and do it.

So that's exactly what I did. A few friends and I piled into a car and drove over to the track. With the rain pouring down and a drone flying overhead (thanks, Iain), I was as ready as I'd ever be. The race went as I expected: with each beer, it got exponentially harder. I got through the first four no problem; it was just like the regular beer mile, but I ran slower knowing I was running double the distance. The fifth beer was a struggle, and by the time I got the sixth down, the beers started coming back up, so I had to pull over for a second and earn my penalty lap. Two more beers and three laps later, I crossed the line in 14:14. *I had broken the world record!* When Phil ran over with the camera to tell me the good news, the only words that came out of my mouth were, "I wouldn't recommend anyone doing that."

Once I had the beer two-mile under my belt, surely the beer mile would be a breeze, right? It was the beer mile equivalent of running a full marathon in preparation for a half-marathon. (However, I've never heard of anyone doing that, probably because it's a bad idea.) Regardless, my confidence was high going into filming the final episode. That episode was what the whole series revolved around: a sub-five minute attempt. We invited all of our close friends to the local track to take part, or at least spectate, in the series finale.

It was the biggest beer mile we had ever organized, and the best part was that for 90 percent of the competitors, it was their first time. All of them had run a mile at some point, and drinking four beers wasn't uncommon for a college student. How would putting them together go? They were about to find out. It was an incredible day for a race: blue skies and virtually no wind; we got lucky. With a good audience out to watch as well, I was excited to give it a crack. Given my previous best was still 5:19, breaking five minutes wasn't likely, but I was definitely ready to run a personal best and wanted to shave off every second I could.

Shirtless but with the green cape tied around my neck, of course, I put all my training to work over the next five minutes. The beers went down fairly smooth and while my legs weren't quite ready for a breakout performance, I crossed the line faster than I ever had before: 5:14. It was a personal best, but I was far from satisfied. I felt that I wasn't aggressive enough with the running early on. Beers three and four weren't super smooth. While a sub-five minute performance wasn't a guarantee, 5:14 was not a fair representation of where I was at. Comments on Trackie.ca reinforced my confidence: "If Kent gets on a surfaced track, puts on spikes, and drops the cape, there is no reason he can't be the next to break 5," said one commenter. One of Canada's top marathoners, Rob Watson, followed with, "That was awesome. Love the technique used to measure the empties. Keep pushing, sub-five is definitely possible under a better racing setup—spikes and a real track." Unfortunately, it wasn't all positive. As expected, there was also this comment: "Wait. Wasn't this called the road to sub-five?"

Luckily, the road wasn't quite over yet, as a few days later I was invited to the Toronto Spring Beer Mile, which was coming up in less than two weeks, right in between two of my exams and near my hometown. I had told the friend that invited me that I was done with the beer mile for a few months but thanked them for the invite. A few days later, I received a Facebook notification from the event page that showed the custom "Toronto Spring Beer Mile 2015" shirt that would be handed out to the winner, along with the usual bragging rights. The shirt looked so cool, and unless a world-class performance came out of nowhere, it was already mine. It's funny looking back on the decision: all it took was a $15 t-shirt to convince me to take a two-day hiatus from studying. Of course there was the extra incentive of inching closer to that five-minute barrier that I cared about way more than any exam. *Sorry Dad.*

Having received a lot of negative comments online after my previous races, I was determined to silence any doubters of my abilities. It seemed extreme: I needed someone to film the entire race as well as someone to show my beers were finished, and I didn't have my roommates handy. Luckily, my brother, Jordan, was around for the weekend, and while I knew my Dad wouldn't want to come, I convinced my Mom to tag along. (I wouldn't say my Dad hated the beer mile, it just took a long time for it to grow on him. Could it have something to do with thinking it was taking away from my studies? *Nonsense.*)

The race was on a Saturday, so as we had done so many times throughout our childhood, Jordan and I sat on the couch and watched TV all morning. However *The Flintstones* were now replaced with ESPN highlights. The afternoon rolled around, and I still had to grab my beer for the race. The night before, Phil had texted me saying that he had found another potential beer that met the strict requirements, Amsterdam Blonde. I drove to the store and just by looking at the blonde color of it, knew it would be a way better choice. The Muskoka Cream Ale I had been using was thick and had a strong taste; a blonde beer sounded like heaven. I grabbed a six-pack and headed home.

The race was about thirty minutes from my parent's house, so I spent the entire drive with a giant beer cooler between my legs to make sure the bottles were kept nice and cold.

When we arrived at the track, I was shocked by the number of people who were there. Between runners and spectators, there must have been close to one hundred people present. It was awesome. The participants were a combination of three Toronto running groups that came together to do beer miles four times a year and had been doing so since long before I had even had my first beer.

Approaching the track, I dropped my stuff and jogged a few laps to warm up. As I stopped, someone yelled out, "Three minutes until we start!" I quickly switched into my flats and did a few strides. Jordan was set up with camera and stopwatch in hand, and my mom was ready to grab the beers to show they were empty. I wanted to get as close to five minutes as possible, and the only way to do that was to go for it from the start. *Could I blow up? Definitely.* But I would rather leave the track knowing that I tried and failed than never tried at all.

Adrenaline was rushing through my veins as the entire group counted down together, "THREE, TWO, ONE!" The sound of dozens of beers opening and the carbonation rushing out had become a familiar one. The first beer went down so smooth: the lighter taste and texture made it a lot easier to chug. It was a blessing in disguise that I had been training with the Muskoka Cream Ales for months; the Amsterdam Blonde went down like water. Even better, the conditions were perfect: a warm spring day with no wind. I took off like a bat out of hell. I grabbed my second beer as a few still struggled to drink their first. Jordan yelled out, "70!" I was on target. Even with the quick pace, I felt surprisingly smooth through lap number two. With such a big group, the rest of the race I was forced to run wide and dodge in between runners as I made my way around the track. While I ran extra distance, it was nice to have people to chase. As I grabbed my final beer, I heard Jordan call out a time but wasn't paying attention to it. I finished the rest of the race and leaned across the line as I heard Jordan call out "5:05!" Excellent, another nine seconds down.

There was quite a range in finishing times, so about twenty minutes later, the final runner jogged towards the line with only a penalty lap standing between him and finally finishing the beer mile. What happened next was strange. Everyone started running with him. Slightly confused, I joined in. It turned out it was event tradition that everyone ran the penalty lap with the final competitor. It was a pretty cool touch.

Enough time had passed that I started to feel tipsy as my mom, Jordan, and I started packing up our stuff getting ready to leave. An announcement went out: "Everyone listen up! It's time to give out our event champion t-shirts and trophy!" In the thrill of the moment, I had forgotten about the t-shirt altogether!

Before calling me to the front, I was introduced by the race director as if I were a god among mortals; a world-class athlete that happened to show up at this community beer mile. That's not how I saw it at all, but I guess they wanted to build up the hype. I was given the custom dry-fit "Toronto Spring Beer Mile 2015" t-shirt and handed the trophy: someone's old running shoe that had been spray-painted gold and glued onto a wooden platform. On it, were all the signatures from previous winners. I was handed a permanent marker, and just like that, my name was forever inked into the event's history. It still is the most unique award I have ever received.

# CHAPTER 8

# The Road to World Champion

FILMING WHAT IT took to be one of the best beer milers in the world was fun, but it was time to move on. I was happy to be ranked fourth all-time and felt like a low-key celebrity within my friend group. But I was still a student and had to take three more exams, so the exciting evenings of chugging and running were replaced with long, boring days spent in the library. Don't get me wrong, I enjoyed school. However, when compared to everything else going on at the time, it was a little tedious. Nonetheless, my intentions to pursue a career in physiotherapy demanded good grades, so the study grind resumed.

Since it was exam season, the training group thinned out as everyone's schedule was thrown off between studying until the early hours of the morning and taking the tests themselves. One day, a group of us had decided to meet at 8:00 p.m. to work out as that was the most convenient time that given day. Torrential rain poured down all day with winds strong enough to lift people off their feet. The awful weather was reflective of the workout to come: a thirty-five-minute tempo run. As we waited for the last few guys to show up to the track, I got a text from a friend asking if I wanted to come over for a study break: a.k.a. watch an NHL game over a few beers. It was days like that which really made me second guess if it was all worth it. I could be sitting on a couch right now sipping on a cold beer while watching the hockey game instead of spending the better part of two hours out in the cold rain. As I declined, I wondered, *Why was I doing this again?* My train of thought was interrupted when a Facebook message request appeared on my phone. I opened up a message from a man named Nick MacFalls with the most intriguing introduction I have ever experienced.

"From a competitive standpoint . . . you want to exert maximum pressure on each competitor . . . Social pressure to run for your country. . . Mental pressure to ensure you finish the beer . . . and physical pressure that could lead to puking or a slower chug. Gallagher showed he's a gamer, but how will the Aussies fare? How will Nielsen run . . . and will his fast chugging put pressure on the field?" I shrugged, perplexed, and decided to revisit the message later as we took off for our run. That evening, after some clarification from the man himself, I got to know who Nick MacFalls was. He was planning the second ever international beer mile in San Francisco, where instead of crowning an individual champion, the goal would be to crown the best beer miling nation in the world. The team-style competition would take place in late August featuring athletes from the United States, Canada, and Australia. With my recent rise in the beer mile rankings, I was all for it.

As spring rolled into summer, I split my weeks between volunteering in physiotherapy clinics and working for a student-run window cleaning company. My only goal in terms of running was to make sure I was healthy and injury-free for the upcoming cross country season that fall.

Because of the way my season was structured, I took time off the last week of June, which was earlier than usual as the summer track season ran until late July. I knew I had the Beer Mile World Classic at the end of August, so I decided to take a break early and give myself seven weeks to build some decent cross country fitness for the race, as well as for the upcoming season. The first two weeks were just easy mileage, getting back into the rhythm of getting out the door to log the daily miles. My training routine still included a lot of cross training—about eight hours of pool running and biking throughout the week.

About six weeks before the race, it was announced that Corey Gallagher was injured and unable to compete at the Beer Mile World Classic. I was extremely disappointed. I was hungry to get back on the line with the best in the world. However, the competition would still be fierce with world-record holder James Nielsen and Australian standout Josh Harris both toeing the line. The announcement of Gallagher's injury also took a huge toll on Team Canada as we would no longer be favorites going into the race.

At the end of the previous summer, Phil and I had organized a beer mile for our local running club to celebrate the conclusion of a long season of racing before we all went back to our respective colleges and universities. We decided to have the second annual event two weeks before the World Classic so Phil and I could use it as a tune-up race. It was a week before the event, and I knew my fitness was building, but

I hadn't touched a track or even done any interval training shorter than mile repeats. I was training for ten-kilometer/six-mile cross country races, not a mile. So I went to the track at the end of my easy run to do a few 400 meter repeats and see what I could do. I surprised myself by running a 66-second quarter pretty comfortably. Once I got my legs up to speed, I barely felt the effort. After a handful of repeats, I called it a day and jogged home.

The following week flew by as I volunteered in physiotherapy clinics and trained. I had a lot going on, but the beer mile was always at the top of my mind. I was no longer just the college kid who crossed his fingers hoping he would be invited to race the best in the world. I was *one* of the best and was hungrier than ever to be *the best.*

With six weeks of solid training under my belt, I started visualizing the beer mile itself in the days leading up to the event. I knew I was ready to run faster than ever before. If everything went perfect, I would break five. Would I have enough to break James Nielsen's world record of 4:57? Maybe. I fell asleep with big hopes for the next day. When I woke up, everything spiraled downward. I had received a dozen texts from friends, ranging from, "Did you see what Josh Harris ran?" to "4:56?? Man, you've got your work cut out for you!" *Damn*! I knew I could maybe barely get Nielsen's time in a perfect run, but now the world record was even further away. Every hour of the day I got another message or read a major media article, the biggest one written by *Sports Illustrated.*

I drove over to my friend Joe Kagumba's house, who was also home for the month before heading back to university. Since we were broke college kids, we had offered to clean one of his neighbor's windows for a few bucks. It would at least pay for our beers later that night. Joe was the ultimate hype man, so for the hours we were cleaning, he was lighting a flame underneath me, using Josh's recent world record to fuel the fire. He knew I would be going head-to-head with Josh in exactly two weeks at the World Classic, and used that to get me excited to race. We finished up and had a few hours to spare before heading to the track for our local beer mile. My phone was still blowing up as it seemed the beer mile had gone viral yet again.

I finally pried myself from my phone and headed over to the track only to find two-dozen mothers pushing their babies in strollers. If it hasn't been made abundantly clear already, I should point out that the beer mile isn't exactly a family-friendly sport; there was no way we could have our race with all these moms and kids around. It was a massive problem, and the sun was beginning to set, meaning that it would be difficult to film the race clearly. In all these months, I had learned one thing for sure: if you gave people a reason to doubt, they would doubt. And a pitch-black video wasn't going to convince anyone. The babies had to go! We waited as long as we could and jumped onto the track knowing the kids in the strollers wouldn't remember being present at what I hoped would be a beer mile world record. Hopefully, the parents would think it was cool, or at least be confused long enough not to interrupt the race. (I've heard the hardest job in the world is being a mother to a newborn, so I'm sure they could have used a beer themselves, or four.) There had been a few obstacles in my career, but now there were dozens of them directly in my way. I couldn't help thinking, *Who would puke more that evening, the babies or the beer milers?*

The only goal that day was to run as fast as I possibly

could. I knew I was ready to break five minutes, but could I beat Josh's time? Would the sun stay out long enough? We were about to find out.

Whether it was dodging the baby strollers or the thrill of potentially running out of sunlight, I was off the line like a cannon as soon as the race started. As I grabbed my second beer I heard my split of 67 seconds. *67!*? Obviously I would slow down but I was on pace to break the world record by twenty-eight seconds! I quickly forgot what I had heard and kept up the quick pace. The cool temperature and atmosphere were perfect. Flying around the track I was in a complete flow state. The middle two laps and beers were just a flash before my eyes. As I finished my fourth beer I heard, "3:51!" By no means was I feeling fresh, as I was definitely feeling the fast pace I took the race out with. However, only needing a 68-second final lap, I knew sub-five was in the bag. It was a matter of how far under I could get. Driving my knees and arms the whole way around that final lap, I gave it everything as I crossed the line. "4:55!" I looked into the camera and said, "Going to have to check the video, could be two world records in twenty-four hours. See you in San Francisco."

This was huge. Not only had I had broken the world record, but it had been broken twice within fifteen hours on two different continents. Surely, this was the definition of a global sport. Massive media outlets like *Runner's World* and *Men's Journal* had posted articles on the story by the next day. It was completely ridiculous, and it seemed that the world thought so too. Still, I basked in the glory of being the best in the world for the moment because who knew how long it would last?

Just over a week later, it was time to head down to the race in San Francisco. Although I flew quite frequently, this would be one of my first times flying alone. I boarded my flight and struck up a conversation with the man I was sitting next to. When he asked the purpose of my trip, I was lost for words. Business? Vacation? Both were true. Not sure where to start, I asked, "Have you ever heard of the beer mile?"

I couldn't believe the next words that came out of his mouth. "Oh yeah! Didn't a Canadian guy just set the world record for that?" What were the chances? He was amazed to hear I was that guy; I answered dozens of beer mile related questions, and before I knew it, we had landed. We shook hands and parted ways. I couldn't believe how interested he was in everything, from the smallest details of the race itself to the history behind it. Phil's flight arrived shortly before mine, so I met him at the luggage carousel. As we waited for my bag, I texted Nick MacFalls, who was on his way to pick us up.

Nick's car was filled of excitement the second we piled in. Nick explained to us that San Francisco was pretty much an eight-mile by eight-mile traffic jam, so it was usually quicker to run or bike to get around. I always wanted to visit San Francisco, and I couldn't think of a cooler reason to be there. Nick was the brains behind it all, and he was in an incredibly positive mood, given the fact he had barely slept in the past week. Coordinating all the athletes' travel, setting up the race course, making sure all the permits were in place—he was a busy man. To limit costs, members of the West Valley Track Club, to which Nick belonged, had offered to host the athletes in their guest rooms for a few nights. So Nick dropped us off at Konrad Knusten's apartment. Just by creeping him online, I knew we would get along well with Konrad. He played in a Smiths cover band and had run on a full scholarship at the University of Oregon.

Phil and I had been talking with him for a few weeks and

he had given us the codes to get into his building and unit. We went up the elevator and to the end of the hall, where Phil unlocked the door. It was a nice bachelor pad, with a big TV room and couches to the left and the kitchen to the right. In the back was the master bedroom and across the hall, the guest room Phil and I would be staying in. John Markell, one of the founders of the beer mile, had told us to meet outside Kezar Stadium in a few hours if we wanted to join their group for a run. We figured we would Uber to where the group was meeting, but after a quick look at the traffic, we saw it was not only going to save us money but also time if we ran over.

It was obvious when we arrived outside Kezar Stadium that we were in the right place. A group of forty runners socialized and stretched as they got ready to run. We recognized John at the edge of the group, and he introduced us to a few of his close friends within the club before we took off. Their group had a workout that day in Golden Gate Park, but Phil and I were taking it easy as it was a travel day. Todd Rose, John's good friend who would also be racing at the World Classic, was coming off a recent injury so he took us around the park for an easy scenic run. The park was incredible, with open grass fields, trees taller than buildings, and so many choices for trails that we didn't even know where to start. One of my favorite parts of travelling is getting to see the sights by foot, and there was lots to see in San Francisco.

After the run, we socialized and stretched for a while. It was tradition on a Tuesday for the group to go out for a few drinks, so we went back to Konrad's to freshen up before heading out. It was a quick turnaround; we ate and flew out the door. The bar wasn't very far, so before we knew it, we were walking in the front door. It was dimly lit, and you could barely hear someone speaking two inches from you, the place was so packed. The bar ran along the entire right wall, with tables along the left. We could see the West Valley group in the back and with no clear route to get there, began dipping and dodging between people. There sat John, Todd, and a few others. John asked Phil and me if we wanted a beer. I think you can guess our answer. We walked over to the bar, which had a massive board full of the different beers they had on tap. We were in paradise. Sours, wheat ales, IPAs, double IPAs, even triple IPAs! They were all craft beers too. Still parched from the run, I couldn't wait to get my hands on a beer. After we ordered, John pulled out his credit card and paid. He told us we were his guests, so the beers were on him. *Sweet*! John was a brave man putting his credit card behind the bar and giving access to the best athletic drinkers in the world. He'd come to regret that at the end of the night.

Shortly after, Nick walked in with someone we had yet to meet. I immediately recognized the lean figure of Josh Harris. Only a few short months ago I had watched half-a-dozen videos of Josh racing to try and learn the art of the chug and how he could beer mile so damn fast. Now, within the last two weeks, we had both set the world record and gained international media attention. In a matter of days, we would be going head-to-head for the Beer Mile World Classic title. *How did this happen again?*

The next two days were split between relaxing, getting to know each other, preparing for the race, and seeing everything that the city had to offer. Konrad was a fantastic host and took a few days off work to show us around. Jeff Mountjoy, our good friend and fellow Canadian, arrived later than expected on Thursday, so we decided to wait until the following day to bike across the Golden Gate Bridge. Usually, I am as lazy as possible the day before a race. I'll do the bare minimum I need to do, and apart from that, I'll be on the couch or lying in bed resting up. However, this was the trip of a lifetime, so the next morning, we got up and went to the bike rental store.

Our bike ride took way longer than we thought, leaving us only twenty minutes to do our shakeout run before we had to go to the athlete meeting at John's. Jeff, Phil, Konrad, and I threw on our running clothes and shoes quickly and hit the roads. I usually like to keep my pre-race run on easy terrain at a slow pace—save the legs for the race. That wouldn't be the case for this run, as every direction led to massive hills. As we climbed yet another incline, I jokingly accused Konrad of attempting to sabotage the Canadian team by taking us on this tough route. He mentioned a marathoner he had heard of who would always warm up by running the steepest inclines within sight: may as well get the body ready by getting the burn going early. That mindset seemed crazy to me, but we ran up those hills anyway.

By the time we got back into Konrad's apartment, we were already late, so the turnaround was even quicker than before. We got into Konrad's car and made our way over to the meeting.

Despite our rush, as we pulled up to John's house, we were in awe. It was massive, like something you would see on *MTV Cribs*. Just inside the door everyone was socializing, with beers in hand of course. I scanned the room and saw a few familiar faces. On a couch sat Michael Cunningham and Jim Finlayson, second and third respectively at the FloTrack World Championships. Standing on the other side of the room laughing away were the elite women, including former world-record holder Chris Kimborough. It was crazy. From a glance, this looked just like your average get together. But it was really a meeting of the best athletes in the world at a bizarre, but rapidly growing, sport.

Walking in, John was happy to see the rest of his Canadian squad show up, and after greeting us, he offered us a beer. We weren't going to say no, especially not to the man who not only funded our travel across the continent but also was footing the bill for the whole event.

As the scheduled meeting was about to start, a roar erupted from the American men, in response to their ace athlete, James Nielsen, walking through the door. Seeing him for the first time in person, I understood why they called him "The Beast." Standing about 6-foot-3, he was built more like a boxer than a distance runner. Fortunately, I would be lining up next to him on the start line, not across from him in the ring. It looked like he had shaved about fifteen pounds in upper body weight since his world record video. This could be big trouble for me and the Canadian team if he was now in better racing shape. He took a seat, and the meeting began.

Nick and John spearheaded the meeting and went over a quick agenda. The laidback mood in the room shifted to a serious silence. They thanked everyone for making the trip to San Francisco, with particular note to the Australians who had traveled for over a day to be part of this special event. Nick and John quickly went through the schedule for the day, then handed out custom national race kits. My Canadian team singlet was white with the iconic red maple leaf in the center with "Beer Mile" written in the middle. In matching fashion, we Canadians were given a pair of red and white paneled split shorts. I had been looking forward to the race for weeks, but that was the moment it really set in. In less than twenty-four hours, representatives from the best beer miling nation in the world would be crowned as champions. I snapped out of my daydream when they began discussing the rules.

About a month earlier, Nick MacFalls had told me he wanted to adopt my clear-cut measuring technique; he declared it the Treaty of Kent. Every athlete would have a handler waiting for them at the end of the chug zone to grab and measure their empty beer. "Did everyone see Lewis's 5:05? Did you see how that lady grabbed and measured out his beer right away?" I laughed because "that lady" was my mom, who agreed to help out that day as long as she was kept out of the video. *Oops.*

FloTrack did a great job with their event by implementing a system so the athletes would finish their beer, but it was a bit complicated. This rule was simple. Every athlete would have a beaker with a red line drawn at four ounces. Your handler would grab every one of your finished beers and place them on a table. At the end of the race, the remnants of all four would be poured into the same beaker. Stay below the line? You were good to go. Anything above the line? Disqualified. After a few clarifications, everyone reached a consensus that it was fair, and the meeting finished.

There was a handful of media at the meeting to gather more details before reporting on the event, including a crew from ESPN. It had been rumored for weeks that they may show up to the race—I guess the beer mile really was gaining some serious traction. I got called down for my individual interview with ESPN writer Greg Garber. The basement was the closest thing I had seen to a professional filming studio. There were four cameramen plus a guy holding that weird stick with a fluffy thing on the end. (I've been told since that it's called a boom.) I thought back to what my coaches had told me growing up, but they hadn't prepared me for this! The interview was focused on how I thought the individual race would play out between James, Josh, and me. I was confidently honest, saying it was any man's race to win, but if I had to put money on it, I would be the first one across the line. It was followed up by a more low-key interview of the entire Canadian men's team with Tim Cigelske of *DRAFT* Magazine. We knew we were the underdog, and acknowledged we would be behind early. We told him our strength would be the latter stages of the race, especially on the beers. He was amazed by the level at which I had studied the beer mile and all the training I had put in for the race.

Our team left filled with excitement and hope for the next day. Shortly after getting back to Konrad's apartment, we decided to head to bed. One final sleep: it would be all business from when we woke up until that gun went off.

I slept like a baby, as I quite often did the night before a race. A lot of athletes struggle with sleep close to competition, as they get nervous and start to overthink everything. All the hard work had been put in, there was nothing that could be done now. *Why set yourself up to fail by stressing about all the little things?*

The day passed by quickly as I relaxed and went over my race plan in my head. The course wasn't going to be smooth. It wasn't hosted on a track as all the local facilities were owned by the city, high schools, or colleges: none of which were willing to take the risk of this crazy, unknown event. Instead, it was hosted on Treasure Island, an artificial island in San Francisco Bay. The loop would be a combination of road, parking lot, and a grass field. While it would slow down the race and make running a world record extremely difficult, maybe it would be exactly what I needed to win this thing.

We arrived at the venue a couple of hours before the race,

as we were instructed. The atmosphere was incredible. John and his team had set the event up as a day-long lawn party, and well over a thousand people had shown up. I found an open patch of grass and lay down to relax. Before I knew it, it was time to warm up. The two weeks since I had set the world record passed in the blink of an eye, and in a matter of minutes, I would once again be chugging and running against the best in the world.

The entire field lined up about 50 meters back of the start line. I was standing second from the inside. To my left, on the very inside, was the legendary Jim Finlayson. Just when the atmosphere felt as professional as ever, the silliness of the beer mile came out as the announcer with his orange suit, big fake afro, and sunglasses stepped to the floor. He picked up the microphone as Jim jogged up, and they called him the "Ol' Gastric Ghost." I couldn't help but chuckle. "And next up . . . your current world record holder from Canada, LEWIS KENT!" I jogged up to the line giving some high fives to the crowd that was lined up on the inside of the race course. I shook Jim's hand and wished him a final good luck. He replied, "I'd say the same, but you don't need the luck." He was so confident I was going to win, I couldn't believe it.

Josh Harris was called up next, followed by the rest of the field. The call up that stands out in my memory is Charlie Blanche, an Australian. He stood in a silk boxing warm-up robe that had the Australian flag printed on it. As his name was called, he tossed it off and underneath he was wearing his Australian beer mile singlet with a pair of women's bun huggers (pretty much bikini bottoms). It was a miracle he got through the race without exposing himself.

They instructed us to grab our beers, and all the athletes bunched up on the line. The three top seeds, Josh, James, and me, were lined up next to one another. I didn't think it would be possible, but not only were there more spectators here than in Austin, but they were also even more enthusiastic. Most of the spectators in attendance actually knew what the beer mile was, and many had taken part in their own earlier in the day. "Whitehorse! My money is on you!" I heard from somewhere in the crowd. As nothing in the beer mile can ever be done as expected, instead of putting our last names on our race bibs, Nick MacFalls had given us nicknames. Mine was Whitehorse: the English translation of the Spanish phrase *Caballo Blanco*. This referred to Micah True, from the narrative memoir *Born to Run*, who stuck out as a tall white man while running with a Mexican ultrarunning tribe. I guess Nick saw a resemblance? I decided to just roll with it.

I had reviewed my race plan over a dozen times on the flight down and the night before. At that point, putting me on the start line with a beer in hand was like putting Kobe Bryant on the free-throw line with a basketball. As close to a sure thing as you can get. I had practiced chugging so many times that I didn't even have to think about it: it was automatic. However, a few other guys in the field had the ability to drink just as quickly, so I imagined there would be a group closely bunched together off the start line. With Josh and James in the field, I guessed the three of us would separate by the second beer. From there I would see how I felt, keeping the pace quick but making sure to keep something for the final two laps. It would be risky to take the lead from the gun as there were gusts of winds reading upwards of thirty miles per hour, but if we were still together as a group after beer number three, my plan was to put in a really hard lap. I had to be in the lead going into the fourth beer and lap if I wanted to win. They both had mile personal bests almost ten seconds faster than mine, so I would get swallowed up if it came down to an old-fashioned sprint to the finish. Still, I had thought of a few other ways that it could play out as well and felt pretty prepared for anything.

"THREE, TWO, ONE!" The whistle went off, and as I had done so many times that year, I twisted the cap off my Amsterdam Blonde and brought the bottle to my lips as I walked to the end of the chug zone. The chug was perfection, with no foam or leftover; I handed it to my handler and took off. I was in the lead and wasn't sure if I was happy about it. I took off down the back straight at a quick but comfortable pace. I turned the corner onto the grass portion and, heading into the home straight, could hear the rest of the field only a few steps back. I slowed down as I grabbed the second beer, and after a big exhale I chugged back beer number two in one go. While most of the field was able to drink it in one chug as well, I had saved precious seconds by not wasting any time between grabbing the bottle and starting to chug. By the time Josh had finished his beer, I was twenty meters in the lead.

As I turned onto the back straight for the second time, a strong burst of wind hit me head on. I pushed hard into the wind knowing that if the pack caught me, my chances of winning were slim to none. I resisted the temptation to look back, tucked my head, and pushed onward. After a smooth third beer, I took a brief look over my shoulder. I had completely broken the field. The only person that now stood between me and my first international title was myself. I stopped to grab beer four and took an extra breath than usual. The hundreds of practice chugs. The late nights at the track with nobody in sight but Greg and his stopwatch. I was twelve ounces and 400 meters from being crowned champion. *Get it down clean Lewis, you've got this*, I told myself. All of the training had paid off, and surrounded by over a thousand screaming spectators, I polished off my last beer. Usually at this point I'd give it everything, leave it all out there to shave off precious milliseconds, but not this day. Although I hadn't heard a single split time all race, I certainly was not on world-record pace. Strong winds and tough terrain made it hard to run fast, but the time was irrelevant. I was there to win. Halfway around the final lap, I did one final shoulder check. That was the moment I knew I had won. I swung wide off the final turn to give the spectators some celebratory high fives. Adrenaline pumping through my system, I threw my hands overhead as I crossed the line in pure ecstasy. In that moment, there couldn't have been a happier person on Earth.

As they ushered me onto the stage for a live interview, it was announced that Team USA had won the team title. Jim had finished strong in third place, but we hadn't done enough as the depth of the United States pulled through. However, by the time my interview was over, Nick MacFalls came over and whispered into the announcers' ears. James Nielsen, who had initially finished sixth, had been disqualified for too much leftover beer! That moved Jeff Mountjoy up one spot and the US back one critical point. Team Canada had won!

I got down off the stage, and everyone gathered together at the start line. *What was happening now?* Someone had proposed the idea of a beer 4 x 400-meter relay. Each runner drinks their beer and runs one lap as fast as possible before tagging the next teammate who could then start their beer. I had done this every year at our annual beer mile, and it was amazing to watch. I'd imagine for most people this would sound like punishment, but to the beer miler it was another chance to shine. On the start line, Josh asked if I wanted to go first and race him head-to-head. Obviously disappointed that his race didn't go to plan, he wanted redemption. While this race was a little closer, I managed to just edge Josh on the first leg. By the end, Mountjoy was just barely able to hold off sub-four miler AJ Acosta to bring home the win for Canada.

A few hours after it was all said and done, after I had spoken to all my family and friends, it began to sink in. It was the deepest field in beer mile history—the only three men to break the five-minute barrier all on the same start line . . . and I had won. The only established beer miler absent was Corey Gallagher, the winner in Austin eight months earlier. Would he have beaten me if he had been able to race? I would get my chance to take him on a few months down the road.

After a very late night of celebrating, we were in rough shape the next morning but up at 8 a.m. for a local 5K road race that Nick had gotten us free entry for. Students love free stuff, even if it's painful. We turned on ESPN quickly before heading out the door and were astounded to see that we were on TV! A six-minute highlight video they had recorded from our race the day before was playing every hour as part of the sports reel. National TV! I couldn't believe it.

The 5K race finished in the San Francisco Giants Home stadium, AT&T Park, which we found super cool. Jeff, Phil, and I had all committed to at least trying to run hard for the first mile. We were in a pack of seven or eight runners, mostly high school athletes. By the time we hit the mile mark around five minutes, I was feeling the night before and put on the brakes. I kept up a decent effort but was in no shape to go for a quick time by any means. Jeff slowed to a jog. I didn't think it was possible, but somehow he must have been feeling worse than I was. I watched ahead as Phil stuck with the lead pack as long as he could. How was he doing it? He had probably drank more beer the night before than the three guys he was running with had collectively drank in their entire lives. At the end of the day, the sober teenagers pushed on as the suds-filled night caught up with Phil and dragged him down to a fourth-place finish. Oh well, at least there was no vomit involved.

What a difference twenty-four hours makes. One day standing on top of the world arm-in-arm with a commentator dressed from the wrong decade, the next day trailing in fifteenth place behind a bunch of high schoolers. The life of a world-class beer miler! With the race over, we had to rush to catch our plane.

As I boarded the plane, the sense of anticipation was high for the second annual FloTrack World Championships later that year. Time to trade in the afro wearing announcer for the dancing bananas.

# CHAPTER NINE

# Living the Dream

AFTER WINNING THE Beer Mile World Classic, I had a flurry of friends in the running community reach out to me. A few were well-connected with brands and offered to help get me some support. I told them to pass along my number and email to any rep they knew at every company they thought would potentially be interested in the beer mile. At that point, I would have sold my soul for a free pair of shoes. Unfortunately, even with the media attention the beer mile had attracted, not a single opportunity came to fruition.

Apart from the occasional interview or fan here and there, life went on as planned. I was in the middle of my fourth and final collegiate cross country season, and while I was far from the best over the eight- to ten-kilometer grind, I was in decent shape and hitting personal bests. That's when I got a call from Kris Mychasiw. Apparently my story had been passed through half-a-dozen people before Kris received an email from a high-ranking colleague that read, "What do you think of this kid?" He picked up the phone and called me right away.

After listing a few athletes that he represented, including multiple Olympians, I realized Kris was the real deal. He seemed genuinely curious about who I was and how the beer mile came to be. After about fifteen minutes, Kris told me I had passed. I was confused. *Was this a test?* He told me he never trusts what's on paper and only works with athletes with whom he personally connects. The conversation quickly changed pace as he asked if I was loyal to a certain brand or company. My answer, "I'm extremely loyal to whatever is in my size and on clearance." He laughed and told me he would reach out to his contacts at a few shoe and apparel companies. As he spoke to me, he was drinking a beer out of a glass that he received the previous week in the mail.

He told me it was covered in big writing that said, "Run Happy to Live Lager" with a finish line at the bottom of the glass. I knew "Run Happy" was the slogan of Brooks Running, and while he didn't have any athletes currently with them, he couldn't see a company that branded pint glasses saying no to the opportunity to work with a beer mile champion. "Soon enough the beer mile is going to be known in every household, and when people think of the beer mile, they will think of Lewis Kent. When they think of Lewis Kent, they will think of Brooks." *How full of it was this guy?* By no means did I think he was intentionally lying, but getting me a shoe deal? *The beer mile becoming a mainstream sport, with me as the face of it?* I obviously had my doubts. He said he would be in touch soon.

While sitting in class the following day, a dead silence in

my 150-student lecture was broken when my phone rang. It was Kris. All eyes were on me as I ran out of the room to pick up the call. Kris immediately asked, "What are you doing on Thursday?" He had booked a meeting with the head marketing team of Brooks Canada. I couldn't believe it. "They're interested, just don't mess it up! Haha." He was just kidding around, and for the next few weeks, a day wouldn't go by where I didn't talk to Kris.

Luckily for me, my parents lived a short drive from the Brooks Canada headquarters. When I called them to explain the opportunity and ask if I could get a ride home, they were totally on board. Heck, I even got to skip two days of classes— it was better than an elementary school field trip.

The meeting was very similar to when I first spoke to Kris. The Brooks team knew all about the beer mile but was curious as to how I got involved in it and the direction I thought the sport was heading. They told me all about their "Run Happy" philosophy and that they had been looking to get involved in the beer mile market for a little while. When the meeting wrapped up, they said they would get back to me shortly with a decision.

Kris called me a few days later to say that Brooks had put an offer on the table to make me the first professional beer miler in history. While the details of the contract are confidential (under penalty of death [okay not really]), Kris said there were only a handful of distance runners in Canada with better deals. This man was a miracle worker! The FloTrack Beer Mile World Championships were still just over two months away, so we decided to wait on making the announcement. Doing it closer to the event would make it more relevant and hopefully grab a few meda headlines. Apart from my closest family and friends, I wasn't allowed to tell a soul.

Every day seemed to be packed between beer mile excitement, training, and schoolwork, but I looked forward to every night as my roommates would always get together at the kitchen table for some cards before bed. It was a nice way to end the day: with a cold beer in hand and more trash talk than any of us could keep up with.

I was grateful to have some great roommates. They had been there every day through the crazy transition from ordinary student athlete to world champion. However, it was hard to keep the two worlds apart. My next collegiate race was at a Division I meet at the University of Louisville and the field was incredibly deep. My ordinary ability was easily demonstrated with a two-hundreth place finish in the race; however, the only two runners interviewed by FloTrack after the race were the winner and myself. After a few basic questions, they asked how fast I was ready to run in Austin, which was quickly approaching. I don't know where the confidence came from after finishing almost dead last in the race, but I boldly told them I would be ready to break 4:50 by the time the World Championships rolled around. *What the heck did the 199 runners that just beat me think of that?*

I had expected the next big announcement in the beer mile world to be my contract, so I was taken off guard to come back from a run the following week to find out that Corey Gallagher had broken my world record, lowering it to 4:54.4. I was disappointed, knowing there wasn't much time left to try and reclaim it, seeing there were only seven weeks to go before the World Championships.

In another surprise, a few days later, FloTrack announced a change in the prize structure. The original prize money was the same, $2,500 for the win and an additional $2,500 if the world record was broken in the race. However, now if the world record was not broken, whoever retained the record would be awarded $1,000, even if they finished dead last. Not that it was all about the money, but I wasn't complaining now that there was even more incentive to reclaim the world record before heading down to Austin.

Money aside, it would be a huge psychological advantage to be the world record holder going into the World Championships. FloTrack, as well as most of the running community, was already betting on Corey since he had won the previous year and had proven he could stay composed under pressure. I knew if I could somehow rebreak the world record close enough to the race, I would be able to get in his head. Even if I put the smallest bit of doubt in his mind, that could be the difference maker in who would be crowned world champion. On November 17, exactly two weeks to the day of the World Championships, Phil and I hit the track for a beer mile time trial. We hadn't run one since San Francisco in August. Worst case, it was a rust buster. Best case, I would get back the world record. Despite some heavy winds, four minutes and fifty-one seconds later, I would recapture the world record.

This was the moment that all great sponsors look for. It was perfect timing to announce that I had become the first professional beer miler in history, signed by Brooks Running. The gamble that Brooks Canada had taken on me only took a matter of weeks to pay off as the video of me rebreaking the world record went viral within an hour of being posted online. I thought my phone was going to explode. ESPN, *Sports Illustrated*, TMZ, The Discovery Channel, Mashable, *Huffington Post*, and *Runner's World*. The headlines read, "This Runner Got an Endorsement Deal for the Craziest Thing," and "College student paid salary to drink beer and run." The

*Globe and Mail*, a popular Canadian newspaper, wrote an editorial on the beer mile becoming "Canada's next Olympic sport." In the moments and time to come when I started to take it all too seriously, I would reflect on the last sentence of the editorial, "Just run with it, kid." While my buddies and I crazed over getting on Mashable and Total Frat Move, business executives were now drinking their morning coffee while reading about the beer mile.

While I started to turn my attention towards Austin, there were still a few academic commitments I needed to attend to. I knew I had prepared well for my exams; however, I still had to get an extension on my final assignments from three professors. Although I knew that word had got around about the beer mile, I didn't expect one professor's response: "No need to fill out any forms or send me any proof! I saw you on my Yahoo home page this morning." Absolutely insane.

From there, I went on the *Ellen Show* and beat Andy on live television. Shortly after, I missed my flight and had to book one for the next day: the same day as the World Championships.

I didn't think I could sleep at all, but before I knew it: BEEP! BEEP! BEEP! My phone alarm went off. Next, Jordan's phone alarm went off. Finally, a wake-up call from the front desk. It all happened so fast. I jumped out of bed for what would be the longest race of my life, starting at 4:48 a.m. in LA and finishing at 9:57 p.m. in Austin, Texas. Ten things needed to go perfectly to plan, and here's how they went:

- Number one: Get on the damn plane. No Lurch, no traffic, no lost luggage. We were already at the airport hotel, so it would be easy. We just had to walk a quarter mile to our gate. No chugging required.

- Number two: Remember to eat. Every runner knows that the timing of nutrition on race day is critical. Hours away from the biggest race of my life, with dozens of international media watching, there I was at 4 a.m. eating cold, overcooked breakfast sausages in the hotel lobby. *Great fuel for the body.*
- Number three: Don't forget Jordan. Kris and my brother had been critical in keeping me calm, and with Kris now back in Montreal, I'd need Jordan to keep my head on straight. Unfortunately, let's just say he's not a great morning person.
- Number four: Tickets, passport, money. Every trip our family took, those were the three things our parents made sure we had as we went out the door. This trip was no different. Everything else I could acquire along the way, but I couldn't function without those three.
- Number five: Once on the plane, get some sleep. As much as nutrition was important, so was proper rest. Going off of less than five hours of shut eye from the night before, sleeping on the plane was the best I could do. The one positive of having to reschedule was that I now had a direct flight, so I could get solid, uninterrupted sleep.
- Number six: Grab the luggage and get to the hotel as soon as possible. FloTrack had taken another big risk by letting me skip out on their local media build up, although *Ellen* airing the afternoon of the race was probably above and beyond the biggest exposure they could have dreamed of. It was a welcome face to see Ryan Fenton at the airport to pick us both up. Lurch was great, but Ryan was better.

- Number seven: Squeeze in a shakeout run. The timing was perfect as Jim and Phil were going for a short jog just as we arrived back at the hotel, so I tagged along. Jordan took our bags up to the room and I left him with a critical task: Get to the store to buy a loaf of bread and a jar of Nutella.
- Number eight: Nutella sandwiches. After the run and a quick stretching routine, I mowed down two Nutella sandwiches. They had never failed me before as a pre-race meal, so I was hoping they wouldn't let me down this time.
- Number nine: More sleep. Please let me sleep. I would need to forget that as I was sleeping, *Ellen* was broadcasting on TV across North America. As I rested, my phone blew up as all my friends and their Ellen-superfan moms tuned in to watch.
- Number ten: Wake up at 6:45 p.m. to catch the 7:15 p.m. shuttle to the race.

And there I was. Despite some speed bumps, everything had fallen into place. Now for the race.

The race was rapidly approaching, but instead of being anxious, I was thrilled. Even with all the curveballs, I still had a great chance at the world title, and all I could think of was Ellen's question from the day before, "So when do you throw up?" That made me laugh and relax. As funny as it would be to have a clip of me vomiting during the race, that had never happened before. Please not now.

The race was held on a quarter-mile loop in the parking lot of the *Austin-American Statesman*, the major local newspaper. Like the previous year, there was a VIP area that only elite athletes and officials were given access to, so Jordan and

I headed there. I hadn't seen a majority of the elite men and women since the summer, and they all had a million questions about *Ellen*. I was glad to answer them but kept my answers short. It was time to get in the zone; there was a night full of socializing ahead.

The open heats had begun well before we arrived, giving the FloTrack team a chance to test the live feed before the championship races. An hour before the elite women's race began, they interviewed the reigning champion, Corey Gallagher.

The race had been hyped up as a head-to-head battle between Corey and me. World champion trying to defend his title against the up-and-coming world record holder. Our personal bests were over ten seconds quicker than the next fastest man in the field, so if one of us didn't cross the line in first, it would be an absolute upset. Then again, it was the beer mile. Anything could happen.

Just over a month prior, Corey had broken the world record with a time of 4:54, just for me to take it back with a 4:51. When the announcer tried to stir Corey up by asking how he felt going into the race not being the favorite, he stayed composed. He said that running a time trial alone was completely different than lining up against the top ten guys in the world. I agreed; what we had done up to this point was irrelevant. All that mattered was who came out on top today.

I was interviewed next and, as expected, the first question was, "So how was Ellen?" I chuckled since I knew I would hear that question hundreds of times over the next month. I then explained how we missed our flight and only arrived in Austin earlier that afternoon. I was surprisingly calm and relaxed considering the craziness of the last twenty-four hours.

After I stepped down, Ryan Fenton told Corey and I

that we had exclusive access to a bathroom on race site if we needed it before the race. There was only one other person that was allowed to use it: Lance Armstrong. Lance had tried a beer mile a few weeks before, and FloTrack was all over it, hoping to add a celebrity presence to the race. Unfortunately, Lance found it more of a challenge to chug beer than cycle the steep slopes of the French Alps. It was cool to hear he would actually be there to watch.

After the interview, it was time to warm up. With a few other elite men, I ran an easy two miles around the race course. We mindlessly bantered on about everything but the race that was edging closer and closer, but underneath the laughing and socializing, my focus was sharp. The last few weeks, through all the training, media frenzy, even *Ellen*, I never took my eyes off the prize. Had the preparation been perfect? Far from it. But I was determined to go out there and give it 100 percent. I was confident going in, having broken the world record twice in less than three months, that I could execute the perfect race plan. At the end of the day, that's all I could do. If Corey was about to run the best beer mile of his life and win by a landslide, I couldn't control that. So I focused on what I could control: running my own race.

I did my warm up stretches, just as I had done a thousand times before. I had been told the same thing by every coach I'd ever had: don't change anything on race day. (Although I don't think my sixth-grade track coach could ever have envisioned this scenario.) I jogged by the start line to take my beer out of the coolers provided, fifteen minutes before race start. When I went to find them, they were gone. *Damn it.* A few elites in the field were using Amsterdam, and someone must have mistaken mine for theirs. Luckily, there were still four scattered across the cooler. I had flown with ten bottles in my carry-on with my initial flight and also brought extra directly from *Ellen*. Amsterdam must have recently changed their bottles, as three had black caps and the fourth, a white cap. This concerned me, but it was too late now. I subbed out my running shoes for racing flats, and after a few strides, we were called to the start line.

From the elite athlete pen, we were called out one by one over the massive speakers. "Next up, you may have seen him earlier today on the *ELLEN DEGENERES SHOW*! Lewis 'HOLLYWOOD' Kent!" Looks like I had earned myself a new nickname.

With the race being late in the evening, it was extremely dark out. To counter this, FloTrack had lit the parking lot with floodlights. I had raced once or twice a year on the track under the stadium lights and loved it. It always felt like the whole world was watching. This time, as I stood there on the start line, I looked to my left and saw massive head cutouts of me being held by fans. I looked into the camera. Kris, my family, and friends would be tuned in. This time the whole world *was* watching, and it was my time to show them what I had been training for.

The race started and before I knew it, I was already behind. Corey had a more aggressive drinking style, and I was caught off guard to be second off the line after the first beer. It had been a year since I wasn't the first off the start line. I knew I wanted to lead from the gun, so I ran by Corey within the first hundred meters. An announcement over the speakers said that Corey had been given a warning for his first beer, meaning he had spilled a generous amount. "If he spills again, Gallagher will be disqualified!" echoed around the race course. *Woah, he must be stressing out about that. Imagine if after all this hype he got disqualified! Actually, there's no way they would disqualify one of us, would they? Focus, Lewis! Focus!*

Even though I've watched track and field my entire life, I'd never before been part of a race where a Jumbotron was used so the fans in attendance could see the race wherever we were around the course. On TV, I'd seen dozens of races where the leader peeks up to the screen to gauge how close behind his or her competition is, but I never thought I'd be in a setting where I could do the same. Now here I was every lap taking a look to see if I had broken Corey. Every time I looked, the answer was the same: he was right on my heels.

All my movements were completely automatic at this point. I grabbed beer two, and before I knew it, it was down, and I was running again. One announcer commented, "That was a hell of a beer," and the other following up with, "That was one of the best beers I've ever seen chugged, not that I've seen a lot in my day!"

I have no recollection of the third beer and lap whatsoever. My next memory is having the fourth beer in hand. Over the loudspeaker, "Another outstanding beer by Kent!"

I took off for my final lap, and one last check up to the big projector let me know that the small lead I had was evaporating. I hit 300 meters to go and decided to give it everything I had. With the flight earlier that day, my legs weren't as sharp as I would have liked them to be for the final sprint finish of the race. If Gallagher was able to keep edging closer into the final turn, he would leave me in the dust. All I had to do was keep the gap as long as I could, make him believe he didn't stand a chance. I still had 25 meters on him going into the final straightaway, and while he was gaining ground with every stride, I knew with 15 meters to go he wouldn't

LIVING THE DREAM ᕙ 133

catch me. As I crossed the line, I grabbed the Brooks logo on my front with my left hand and held up the number one with my right hand. "4:47! New World Record! Not even close!" I couldn't believe it.

Jordan had jumped over the barriers and ran into me with a massive hug. I told him I'd have to go congratulate the rest of the competitors and realized he had tears of joy running down his face as I let go. As important as this moment was to me, it was just as big to him. He was proud of his little brother. For me, everything had happened so fast. But for now, I had business to take care of. I congratulated the rest of the field and did a post-race interview with Ryan Fenton. As had happened a few times before, a wave of nausea came over me about ten minutes after crossing the line, while I was in the middle of my interview, so I jogged off camera for a quick reversal of fortune. I knew all my family and friends were still watching, and I didn't want Grandma Kent tuning in from Scotland seeing that.

I was crowded by media and fans with fat heads, so I spent a few minutes signing autographs. An interviewer said, "This time last year you finished fifth in the world. Since then you've broken the world record three times, appeared on the *Ellen* show, and now you're world champion. That must be the best twenty-first year of anyone's life. Plus you're $5,000 richer! Drinks on you tonight?" I laughed it off as none of that would sink in until days later.

There surely couldn't be a higher peak for me. But the spirit of the night was that there was more to come. It was captured in a photo taken post-race with the Canadian and US Brooks team that had showed up to support. A later edit of the photo really rang true, "Kent Stop Me Now."

# CHAPTER TEN

# So What's Next?

A LOT HAD happened in the last fourteen months. Something I saw as nothing more than motivation to get back into running after an injury had gotten me international media attention. First the beer mile had taken me to San Francisco, then Austin, and of course LA for *Ellen*. However, that was only the beginning.

As I mentioned earlier, my professors were all generous enough to move around my assignments and exams to accommodate for my beer mile adventure down to Austin. I knew when I arrived back I had some catching up to do academically. I got back to my college house late on a Wednesday evening, still feeling the aftereffects of the celebrations from the night before. My roommates had waited up to congratulate me and wanted to hear every little detail. These were the guys who pushed me to try and qualify for the first World

Championships; without them, none of this would have been possible. Their support and energy was what started this whole journey.

After catching up, we eventually called it a night, with the final day of class for the semester being the following day. When I woke up to my alarm at 7:20 a.m., it was like everything was back to normal: time to get up, shower, eat, and catch the bus to class. I walked into the lecture hall and sat down in my usual seat. As my friends sat down around me, each one had a few questions about the trip. As I was mid-answer, our professor began speaking. "For today, I have a lecture prepared covering the last piece of new content for the final exam," he declared. Everyone hushed quiet and gave their attention to the front. "However, if you didn't already know, just a few days ago a classmate of yours was across the continent doing something pretty cool." He then proceeded to pull up the video of my race and 150 of my classmates watched along as I chugged and ran to a world title. Funny enough, it was the only professor that didn't give me the extension I had asked for, but he absolutely loved it. His eyes were locked to the screen and he commentated along as the race went on. He screamed as I crossed the finish line as if he were there in person. It was easily my favorite lecture of my undergraduate career and only marked the beginning of exciting things to come.

By the end of the year, I would go on to be publicly voted one of IAAF SPIKES "Personalities of the Year," recognized as an athlete that made 2015 memorable on and off the track. The list was made up of world-class athletes that had overcome serious illnesses, injury, and adversity to still compete with the best of the world. At the top of the list, I was the anomaly. They noted, "Whatever you think about the beer mile, Kent definitely got people talking about track. That can only be a good thing." Being recognized by the sport's governing body was pretty damn cool.

Into early 2016, Kris fielded plenty of sponsorship requests as commercial interest in the beer mile exploded. By the spring, not only was I representing Brooks, I had become an ambassador for five other companies: SOS Rehydrate, Run Gum, Those Canadians, Cold Shoulder Bags, and Wrist & Rye. Worthy of noting is that Nick Symmonds, the US 800-meter Olympian I managed to beat at the World Championships in 2014, is the co-founder and CEO of Run Gum. I had the support of a world-class athlete! Oh, and don't worry, once the free supply of beer from Ellen ran out, Beau's All Natural Brewing Company stepped in with a supply of beers to be savored, not chugged.

Going into the summer of 2016, I signed a deal to be the ambassador of a series of beer miles all across the country, branded as the National Beer Mile. The owners attempted to commercialize the beer mile, bringing the event to every major city across the US. No longer would it just be the top athletes in the world duking it out for glory; they wanted recreational runners to show up with a handful of their friends and compete for their own set of bragging rights. I would go on to compete at National Beer Mile events in Cleveland, Las Vegas, and Buffalo, which hosted the biggest beer mile in history with over 2,000 participants in July 2016. While the series did not continue into 2017, word on the street is it is only a matter of time before the right business model is found and another series succeeds.

That same summer, reveling in the hype surrounding the beer mile, Brooks flew me to Seattle for their summer sales meeting. The event hosted hundreds of employees from around the world. Earlier in the week, professional marathoner and

Olympian Desiree Linden spoke to the entire Brooks team about her training and dedication to the sport. Desi's appearance had been planned weeks in advance, and the staff had been anxiously awaiting her presence.

What none of them knew was that Brooks had scheduled a beer mile as a finale to the long week of meetings. As the last meeting of the week wrapped up, in the closing remarks, the speaker mentioned they had brought a special guest in from Canada and called me to the stage for a quick Q & A.

I felt like a celebrity as everyone I spoke to was so proud to say that Brooks sponsored the only professional beer miler in the world. I even got to meet company CEO Jim Weber, who still inspires me with his positivity and energy. Brooks would go on to sponsor an event later that summer in Washington, DC, that made for another great trip for Jordan and me.

In July, the Beer Mile World Classic went international to London, England. And while it wasn't my day and I was unable to defend my title, Team Canada took home the gold once again in the first professional beer mile on European soil. A few months later, I received a request to speak in Singapore about the benefits of integrating beer as a reward system with exercise. *How much more ridiculous could this get?*

Later in 2016, Brooks would create a custom shoe specifically for me to race in at the FloTrack World Championships: the Beer Mile Hyperion. The level of support I received was above and beyond anything I could have expected. Only three pairs of the custom shoe exist: one in the Brooks headquarters in Seattle, one that I continue to race in, and one fresh pair, with the tags still on them, sitting in my childhood bedroom at my parents' house.

In early 2017, I got to make an appearance at what I can imagine will be my only professional track and field meet ever.

I competed, if you can even call it that, against Olympic 400-meter champion Jeremy Wariner and Rio Olympian Charles Philibert-Thiboutot, both of whom I am lucky enough to remain good friends with to this day. The event was a Pursuit 1200-meter race at the Montreal Grand Prix, run on a tight cornered 200-meter indoor track. The 1200-meter race was an off distance event, and to add to the novelty, increasing prize money was paid out to the leader after every lap, starting at $50 for the first lap up to $1,000 for the final. I had a decision to make: do I run my own race and go for a personal best, or do I run with the pros as long as I can? If you've made it this far, you know me well enough to be confident that I did the latter. It wasn't even 600 meters into the race before my legs tightened up, I fell off the pack and slowed to a snail's pace in comparison to the rest of the field. If I had to do it all over again? I would have run the first lap even faster to try and win the prize money.

It wouldn't stop there, as that May I was invited to Melbourne, Australia to compete in the Brooks International Beer Mile, the first professional beer mile held in the Southern Hemisphere. I competed against Josh Harris before touring around a country I didn't think I would get to see for years, if not decades, into the future. It made for an outstanding race and trip of a lifetime. Melissa Vandewater, the race director, was incredible, showing me the sights around Melbourne in the days leading up to the race. On race day, Josh and I put on a good show for the crowd, and I came away with the win in the fastest beer mile ever run on Australian soil. We both won some Brooks gear and a case of beer. Josh, being a smaller guy than me, was a little giddy on the post-race podium (see photo in the insert).

After the race, I had six days left to see as much of

Australia as I could, so the remainder of the trip was made up of early wake-ups, days full of sightseeing, and flights to the next destination. I made it to Tasmania, Sydney, and Great Ocean Road. I can't wait to go back one day.

However, as with anything in life, with the highs come the lows, and my journey with the beer mile hasn't been perfect. From the moment I signed my Brooks deal to the present, there have been plenty of critics. As the event involves the consumption of alcohol, I was not surprised by some of the backlash, but what did catch me off guard was a handful of semi-professional track athletes that were outraged to hear someone had signed a professional contract to drink and run. While I completely understand their point of view, as track and field is a very poorly-funded sport with only Olympic caliber athletes being offered contracts like mine, I respectfully disagree with their frustration. Furthermore, I'm happy to say that the majority of track and field fans, as well as professional athletes, agree with my take. The beer mile has gotten attention from massive media companies that would never report on track and field, and I believe that brings value back to the sport itself. While people may be more intrigued by the beer portion of the event, it gets them talking about track nonetheless.

This is the age of disruption. Uber. Airbnb. Driverless cars. Markets across the world are being challenged by innovation. The beer mile is no different as it creates a new form of entertainment for both the participant and the spectator. It has taught me that a fun life is one filled with working with creative people. Don't be put off chasing your dreams by the fear of failure, or in this case throwing up. It has taught me that amazing things can happen to ordinary people. If you work hard, amazing opportunities seem to fall right into your lap.

Who knows what could happen next—maybe even a book deal?

As I remain excited about the future of the beer mile, I do just as I did with Corey on my tail that final straight of the World Championships. I look over my shoulder, back at life, and realize that if you try something new and you throw up, it's only a penalty lap anyway.

# Acknowledgments

I SERIOUSLY CONSIDERED writing a second book to thank everyone who made this possible.

First of all, I cannot thank my dad (Gary), mom (Diane), and brother (Jordan) enough for their continuous support in this venture—as well as all others in my life. I am grateful for everything you do for me.

To my agent, Amelia Appel—for taking a long shot on a guy who couldn't get himself to sit down and write a college paper. Thank you for all the good laughs and your hard work over the past three years.

To Caroline—thank you for being by my side every step of the way. I couldn't ask for someone more supportive and inspiring in my life.

To all my family in the UK who have woken up time and time again in the middle of the night to watch my races live.

To Kris Mychasiw—thank you for taking an average college runner and developing him into a marketable, world-class athlete. You took a spark and poured gasoline on the fire. To the rest of the team, I can't wait to see what the future holds.

To all my coaches—thank you for your guidance throughout my athletic and academic career. I will carry the lessons you have taught me for the rest of my life.

To my first ever sponsor, Brooks Running. I'm proud to have embraced the "Run Happy" brand and lifestyle for the last four years. Your ongoing generosity and support is greatly appreciated.

To my editor, Veronica Alvarado—thank you for your attention to detail and for crafting this manuscript into something special.

Finally, to all my roommates and teammates who kick started this wild journey. Thanks for the peer pressure, the good times, and the incredible memories.

#POW